SEPARATE WAYS

PRAISE FOR SEPARATE WAYS

"For an area of life as difficult for a parent to manage as breaking up, it's amazing to me how few books actually provide a holistic overview of what's really going on, or more importantly, insights into how best to manage it all. Then I came upon Separate Ways. Take it from me, this book does. More than that, this is THE book.

Without doubt, Separate Ways is one of best guides on this most thorny of issues that I've ever seen. It covers it all: law, psychology, support, self-care. Do yourself or someone else who needs it a favour; buy this book."

– PETER NICHOLLS, CEO, PARENTS BEYOND BREAKUP

"Shaya's book confirms what her style of practice as a family lawyer already suggested: she authentically values the emotional perspectives of her clients. A lawyer with heart, giving both sensible and thoughtful guidance to those whose hearts are grieving following separation."

– OLIVIA KAY, FAMILY CONSULTANT & FAMILY LAW COURT REPORT WRITER

"As a professional working with individuals and families at a critical point in their lives, it is a privilege to work with and to acknowledge their experience after separation. Shaya has put together so much of what we need to be reminded of in one place. The information in this book is useful for both individuals and professionals and gives us a shared language to use when working together and talking about grief and loss."

– **Roxanne Nathan**, Family Dispute Resolution Practitioner, Child Consultant

"Shaya writes with care and compassion and a clear and experienced voice, giving sound and candid advice for all men and women trying to map their way through the mazes of negotiation and litigation.

Separate Ways offers timely navigational skills and resources for anyone dealing with loss and grief and deserves to be read at every part of the process, not only to understand what's happening to you, but moreover to understand yourself."

– **Brian McQuade**, Family Law Barrister

"Shaya deals with the multifaceted issue of separation, truly sensitive to the needs of those who have separated from their partner, drawing on her own experiences of loss, those of her clients, and the advices of experts in this area, and does so with a holistic and all-encompassing delivery.

I highly recommend this book to those who are or have already separated, litigants, and family specialists alike. No stone is left unturned or unexamined. It is an easy read, written with beautiful sensitivity, and practical and accurate advice."

– ROSE-MARIE READ, FAMILY LAW BARRISTER, LEGOE CHAMBERS

"As a counsellor, I found Separate Ways to be a comprehensive, useful book, written in a personal, warm and intelligent way. Whilst retaining its informative and authoritative edge, drawn from her extensive experience in Family Law, Separate Ways has a human and sensitive tone too.

Shaya demystifies the 'legalese' a client might encounter, making it a less anxiety-provoking experience. She helps make it more approachable and achievable amidst the stress and pain of separation, divorce, and family law wrangles.

I'd recommend this book to both professionals and clients alike. It offers a balanced view of legal issues – including realities and limitations – and discusses the practical, relational and emotional challenges of separation. Shaya suggests a range of supportive, personal habits to foster, which can help weather the storm and assist in making good decisions."

– PAUL ELLIS, COUNSELLOR

Separate Ways: Surviving post-separation grief, the stress of divorce or separation, and the family law process
Copyright © 2020 by Shaya Lewis.
All rights reserved.

Published by Grammar Factory Publishing, an imprint of MacMillan Company Limited.

No part of this book may be used or reproduced in any manner whatsoever without the prior written permission of the author, except in the case of brief passages quoted in a book review or article. All enquiries should be made to the author.

Grammar Factory Publishing
MacMillan Company Limited
25 Telegram Mews, 39th Floor, Suite 3906
Toronto, Ontario, Canada
M5V 3Z1

www.grammarfactory.com

Lewis, Shaya, 1979–
    Separate Ways: Surviving post-separation grief, the stress of divorce or separation, and the family law process / Shaya Lewis.
Includes index.
ISBN: 978-1-989737-06-4

1. LAW038020 LAW / Family Law / Divorce & Separation 2. LAW038000 LAW / Family Law / General 3. FAM015000 FAMILY & RELATIONSHIPS / Divorce & Separation

Production Credits
Printed by McPherson's Printing
Cover design by Designerbility
Interior layout design by Dania Zafar
Book production and editorial services by Grammar Factory Publishing

Disclaimer
The material in this publication is of the nature of general comment only and does not represent professional advice. It is not intended to provide specific guidance for particular circumstances, and it should not be relied on as the basis for any decision to take action or not take action on any matter which it covers. Readers should obtain professional advice where appropriate, before making any such decision. To the maximum extent permitted by law, the author and publisher disclaim all responsibility and liability to any person, arising directly or indirectly from any person taking or not taking action based on the information in this publication.

SEPARATE WAYS

SURVIVING POST-SEPARATION GRIEF,
THE STRESS OF DIVORCE OR SEPARATION,
AND THE FAMILY LAW PROCESS

SHAYA LEWIS-DERMODY

CONTENTS

INTRODUCTION: Post-Separation Loss and Grief are Real
- Grief is an Emotional Response to a Loss
- The Wounded Healer
- This is Your Journey

CHAPTER ONE: You Are Not Alone
- John's Story
- Jane's Story
- Sophie's Story
- Dan's Story
- Jillian's Story
- Amanda's Story

CHAPTER TWO: Understanding Loss and Grief in a Family Law Context
- The Original Theory on Grief
- Forms of Loss in the Context of Family Law
- Your Loss is Significant

CHAPTER THREE: The Stages of Grief, Plus More
- Anticipatory Grief
- Denial
- Anger
- Bargaining
- Depression
- Acceptance

CHAPTER FOUR: Getting the Right Support
- The Family Lawyer
- The Criminal Lawyer
- The Barrister
- Support Groups
- Friends and Family

CHAPTER FIVE: Navigating the Family Law Process
- Going to War: Is it Really Worth it?
- Property Matters
- Parenting Matters
- Following an Agreement or Court Order
- Flaws in the System
- Are Lawyers Partly to Blame?
- Stories from the Frontline

CHAPTER SIX: Taking Back Control
- Take Some Time
- Be Organised
- Where There's a Will, There's a Way
- Arm Yourself with Knowledge
- Wear Your Business Hat
- Mediate and Negotiate (Don't Litigate!)
- Cap Your Legal Costs
- Batch Tasks as Necessary
- Be Grateful (Yes, Really!)

CHAPTER SEVEN: Prioritising Your Mental Health
- Getting Help Could Change Your Life
- Court Considerations
- Knowing When to Reach Out

- Anxiety in Grief
- Dealing with Triggers
- Friends are Not Mental Health Professionals
- Separation and Men's Mental Health

CHAPTER EIGHT: Embracing the Art of Self-Care
- Diet and Exercise
- Drugs and Alcohol
- Sleep and Stress
- Mindfulness and Meditation
- Cry, Baby
- Social Media
- The Family Home
- Other Suggestions

CONCLUSION: An Opportunity to Grow
- Some Days are Just Shit
- You Get to Choose How You Navigate Your Loss

- Helpful Resources
- Acknowledgements
- About The Author

For my Dad (Fatboy) and my Mum (Chrissy).

Life is not the same without you.

INTRODUCTION

POST-SEPARATION LOSS AND GRIEF ARE REAL

A SEPARATION AND DIVORCE CAN BE ONE OF THE MOST TRAUMATIC experiences you ever go through.

They say that every cloud has a silver lining. But sometimes, there simply isn't one (or it doesn't emerge for some time). Life can hurt deeply, and the breakdown of a relationship can be one of the most significant losses you may ever experience.

Have you recently separated? Are you still feeling the emotional impact of your separation and wondering if there is a supposed light at the end of the tunnel?

Perhaps you feel as though the way you are feeling is not 'normal'. Perhaps you are experiencing anxiety, which you have not experienced previously.

Perhaps you feel as though you are alone on this journey of separation and loss. Everyone around you continues to go about their daily lives, while your world has significantly changed. *You* have changed. You will never be the same.

Regardless of whether you were married or in a de facto relationship, you are experiencing feelings of loss and grief since your separation. These feelings are perfectly normal.

This book is not a legal-fee-saving book or a step-by-step legal guide. Rather, this book will appeal to you if you are looking to understand why you are feeling the way you are.

This book is for you if:

- You have recently separated from your ex-partner.

- You had a relatively amicable separation and your communication with your ex-partner is okay.

- You did *not* have an amicable separation. You may or may not be instructing lawyers and you may or may not be in the Family Law Courts. (I sincerely hope that you are not, but many people who have separated find themselves in this position.)

- You want to have a better understanding of the thoughts and behaviour of your ex-partner in order to deal with them more effectively.

- You want tips and practical advice to survive and thrive during this difficult period.

Regardless of the specifics of your situation, you have still experienced a significant loss in your life due to your separation.

POST-SEPARATION LOSS AND GRIEF ARE REAL

You have likely picked up this book because you're struggling with the heavy burden associated with separation. You may feel exhausted. You may feel confused about the next steps. You may not necessarily be in court, but you may be concerned about ending up in the Family Law Court system.

You may or may not have decided to end the relationship. To be honest, it may not particularly matter whether you were the instigator of the separation, as often the feelings that you and your ex-partner are feeling will be similar.

If you did initiate the separation, then you may have even felt a sense of relief at some point! But it does not mean that you have not experienced a loss just because you ended the relationship and/or felt a sense of relief. There will almost always be one person who feels more abandoned or left behind. However, both parties are still likely to struggle with their loss. Both parties will grapple with feelings of grief.

GRIEF IS AN EMOTIONAL RESPONSE TO A LOSS

As a family consultant, Artemicia Nisyrios has many years of experience in the social science arena. When asked whether she considered those who have separated to have experienced a loss in the form of grief, she responded:

> *'I think everyone manages the process of family law separation differently. Some will feel joy and relief from being free from an unhappy and unhealthy relationship. Some may compartmentalise their experiences and*

never acknowledge the grief/loss they are feeling. Some will be so focused on blaming others (i.e. their "ex") that they will remain in the stage of "anger" or "denial" and not acknowledge any grief. The majority, however, I believe, experience a significant loss, one that takes many years to heal and is certainly a form of grief.'

As you'll discover in this book, the emotions that you are feeling are normal. As Artemicia points out, you may be feeling anger, depression, fear or even *relief*. You may also have periods of happiness. You may enjoy new levels of freedom and responsibility that flow from your separation.

You may be scared or have reservations for exactly the same reason. You may think there's nothing worse than reconciliation with your ex-partner. Or you may be hanging on to some hope that, despite the time that has lapsed, there is still a chance to resolve your differences or to reconcile.

Roxanne Nathan is a family dispute practitioner, who previously worked as a coordinator at a children's contact service (where parents spend supervised time with their children). Roxanne agrees that there is certainly a loss that flows on from separation, which can lead to feelings of grief:

'People don't get into relationships to break up.

'... There is a loss of self and identity: – "Who am I if I am not a member of a family anymore?" - for With men I have worked with, they have felt as though they are so often the working parent after children are born. They have shared the loss of their ideas of what it is to be a man: "I put so much into this family. I kept a roof over their heads and I kept everyone fed, and now I have to sell my home.". For the women clients I see, they often share with me their sense of being devalued:, "I was the one who gave up parts of my individuality to have our babies, stay and at home and care for them," and so often their story is one of not feeling seen.

'So often I hear that life experiences are lost... Not getting to see children every day anymore. In high conflict cases, not being able to go to school events or birthday parties and Christmas Day are often losses for the adults and the children of the separated family.'

By better understanding the stages of grief and loss, in the context of a separation, you'll come to understand that it's okay for you to grieve. And while you will read about other people's experiences, it is important for you to do this in your own time and in a way that is right for you.

You may find yourself reading this book from cover to cover. Or it may be too difficult to read and you may need to stop reading at times. You may flick past certain sections but decide to go back to them in a few months' time. Not everything in this book may seem applicable to you right now. This book is not about *fixing* you. It's designed to help you by pointing you in the right direction. And I believe I'm the right person for the job.

THE WOUNDED HEALER

My name is Shaya Lewis-Dermody.

I have been working as a lawyer in the family law jurisdiction for almost twenty years. However, it was not until I first experienced my own loss and grief that I *really* turned my mind to the difficulty that my clients experience when trying to navigate separation and the family law system for the first time. (You might be surprised to learn that even expert solicitors struggle – and they know the family law system inside out).

For the average person, the family law system is perhaps as uncertain and unpredictable as the medical system was for me. I started writing this book while navigating the medical and hospital system over a two-year period on behalf of my terminally ill parents, both of whom have since died.

I consider myself to be a reasonably intelligent person, and I was certainly able to advocate for my dying parents where necessary. What I did not foresee during those two years was my lack of certainty regarding the process and also my lack of knowledge about the medical system in general. This uncertainty was coupled with the immense grief I felt over the death of both of my parents, who died around eighteen months apart. At times, I felt like my life was out of control.

The grief that I experienced through the death of my parents has similarities to the loss and grief suffered through the breakdown of a relationship, divorce, separation from children, and perhaps the loss of what it means to be a family.

It was only during the process of writing this book that I learned about the concept of the 'wounded healer'. The wounded healer is a term created by Swiss psychiatrist Carl Jung. It's based on the idea that those who seek to help others are doing so because they are, in turn, trying to help themselves. For example, think of the number of people who pursue a career in counselling or psychology. Often, they have experienced trauma in their own life, which has influenced their career choice.

Given my experience as a lawyer, I have become very confident drafting documents, dealing with nasty correspondence from lawyers, and stepping into a courtroom. I do not have difficulty navigating the 'system' as I am very confident in that setting. Many lawyers forget that their clients are overwhelmed by the process, particularly when they're also dealing with feelings of loss and grief.

This book is not about *my* grief, although it was the driving force behind writing this book in order to help others. The grief I experienced and continue to experience has simply been the injection of passion that I needed to write the book!

In addition to drawing on my almost twenty years of assisting family law clients, I have interviewed a number of current and past clients in depth to better understand their stories, with a focus on the loss they felt and their coping techniques. I have spoken with mental health professionals, family dispute resolution practitioners (who facilitate mediation), family court consultants, family report writers, staff at children's supervised contact services, and psychologists.

Pete Nicholls, the CEO of Australian suicide prevention service Parents Beyond Breakup (which facilitates the support groups Dads in Distress and Mums in Distress), has also provided invaluable input and commentary. His service supports parents going through separation by keeping them alive and in their kids' lives. There is a real focus on helping people to deal with their feelings of isolation and hopelessness.

THIS IS YOUR JOURNEY

Let's be honest. You probably wish that you weren't reading a book like this. As a family lawyer, it is rare that I have a client attend my office with excitement or enthusiasm to see me. Their hand is often forced, or they feel there is no other option but to protect their assets or get the best advice in relation to parenting matters. None of my clients are particularly happy to see me and most wish they were not there. I don't take that personally – I'm not a massage therapist or selling coffee! When wearing my 'lawyer hat', it is my role to guide clients through the minefield that is family law based on my knowledge and experience. My hope is that this book offers you some similar assurance.

This book was written to help people like you to deal with the emotional and practical issues around separation. I suspect that you are not overly confident navigating what will be your own journey and pathway through our complex family law system. This book is my way of sharing my insights into the family law system, and sharing clients' experiences and tips for surviving it.

I am very grateful to my family law clients (past and present) who have shared their personal stories. Their willingness to open up to me was brave and perhaps therapeutic for them, but it was certainly insightful for me. My interviews are broad – I've spoken to parties who separated on a very amicable basis and where their communication was positive, parties trying to navigate property settlements, and parties dealing with more worrying matters, including allegations of family violence and sexual assault.

One last thing before we move on...

This book is written from a family law perspective and is also shaped by my own personal experience of loss and grief. I do not have qualifications in social science, but I do know the 'system' very well!

I suspect there will be parts of this book that resonate with you and perhaps others that do not. There is no correct way to emotionally deal with our family law system or the loss and grief associated with separation. This is your journey.

CHAPTER ONE

YOU ARE NOT ALONE

I HAVE WORKED WITH THOUSANDS OF CLIENTS, SOME OF WHOM have been interviewed for and have contributed to this book. Their stories are unique, yet they offer many similarities in terms of the feelings of loss and grief following the breakdown of a relationship.

Many of my clients have gone through the most horrendous and litigious family law separations. I have assisted and interviewed clients who have been victims of horrific family violence. I have interviewed and assisted clients who have been victims of parental alienation.

For others, their separation has been relatively amicable, although they have still experienced a strong sense of loss. One example is my friend Simon, who has been able to effectively co-parent with his ex-wife based on a shared care agreement and, with a couple of meetings with collaborative lawyers, divide their multimillion-dollar asset pool. Despite being able to reach such a collaborative agreement, Simon still struggled *severely* following the loss of his relationship.

I also spoke at length with my friend Nicole, who also has

never instructed a lawyer and was able to resolve all issues by agreement with her ex-partner. She even had her ex-partner join herself and their son on an overseas trip!

It is truly refreshing these days to see an increase in the use of collaborative family lawyers, who are working with a genuine intent and focus to resolve family law matters in the kindest way possible. Having been in the industry for almost twenty years, I have certainly noticed an increase in lawyers offering more collaborative approaches in recent years.

But this won't diminish your feelings of loss and grief.

My view is that regardless of whether there has been an amicable division of your asset pool or agreement in relation to children, it is very likely that you are still feeling a true sense of loss. Even those situations can cause a level of stress. And even though you may be 'peacefully' navigating your family law matter, you're likely still experiencing grief from your separation.

Perhaps you are at the other end of the spectrum, in that you and your ex have not been able to reach an agreement about *anything*. There may be Apprehensive Violence Orders. There may be no communication whatsoever with your ex-partner. It may be that you feel alienated by your ex-partner, who is not enabling you to spend sufficient time with your children. The reality is that many people going through a separation and experiencing a loss are simply unable to reach an agreement on much at all.

Even though your journey is unique, you likely have at least two things in common with other people who have gone through a separation:

1. You did not anticipate that you would be in this situation, and
2. You are experiencing a sense of loss.

Going through a separation can feel incredibly lonely. But one of the most important things to remember is that *you are not alone*. Many people have stood where you now stand, feeling the way you feel.

For the remainder of this chapter, I'd like to share the stories of some of the clients I interviewed for this book. I think it is important to share the stories and struggles of others throughout their separation to help you understand that you are not alone in terms of the feelings that you have and your sense of loss. Sharing other people's stories can help you to realise that while every single separation is unique, there are also a number of similarities.

All client names have been changed, as have some minor details, so as to maintain anonymity. This won't be the only time you'll hear from these people, though. I'll refer to their respective journeys, and their tips and recommendations, throughout this book.

JOHN'S STORY

John reluctantly approached my law firm for some legal advice after he separated from the mother of his two children. It had been a relatively long relationship of over ten years and the separation was very amicable.

Having worked hard for many years, often doing hard physical labour, John had been able to establish himself financially, owning and maintaining property in his sole name, despite not being on 'mega bucks'.

John described his communication with his ex-partner as positive post separation and said they had been able to resolve their property division by agreement. Both John and his ex-partner appeared to me to be extremely courteous and reasonable. They had largely reached an agreement without solicitors and wanted us to draft their property settlement so as to ensure it was watertight.

Despite John's separation being amicable, this did not lessen his sense of loss following the breakdown of his relationship. He had stayed in the relationship for at least a year longer than he wanted to, as he wanted to be with his children. He could not bring himself to leave the family home.

Once he left, he found that he was regularly experiencing depression as he was no longer living in the family home with his children. He started drinking alcohol to excess, which was out of character for him. He felt a sense of helplessness and felt anger towards his ex-partner as he was not able to see his children daily.

JANE'S STORY

Jane was a school teacher and came to me after her separation from her husband of some fifteen years. He was also a professional person and they were both employed on a full-time basis. They had one daughter together and it was apparent that both Jane and her ex-partner thought the world of her and wanted the best for her.

Jane spoke to me about her initial feelings post separation, particularly when it was apparent that she might end up with a battle on her hands. She explained to me that she did not have any friends or family members who had ended up in the Family Law Courts or had faced a 'serious' custody battle. Nobody that she was directly connected to had been through such a bitter separation dispute.

Unfortunately, Jane found herself in a high level conflict situation when she decided to leave her marriage. She initially tried to stay in the family home post separation for the sake of her daughter. However, it became apparent that it was not feasible for that arrangement to continue.

It essentially became a 'standoff', with neither Jane nor her husband willing to leave the family home so as to 'give up' their custody rights of their daughter. Both wanted their daughter in their respective care on a full-time basis. Jane was desperate to co-parent and to share the care of their daughter. However, her husband was insistent on their daughter living with him. The situation quickly found Jane involuntarily in the Family Law Court system.

As she said to me, *'People like me don't end up in this situation... This sort of stuff doesn't happen to me.'* She also spoke about another teacher who had gone through a nasty breakup and had set her ex-partner's car on fire. Even she didn't end up in court! Jane then went on to ask me, *'How the hell did I end up in this situation?'* Good question.

SOPHIE'S STORY

Sophie came to me after spending a few months instructing another law firm and having quickly accumulated some $50,000 in legal fees (which, in my view, was excessive based on the work completed).

In a relationship for seventeen years, Sophie and her husband had two young children together. She had a motor vehicle accident prior to living with her husband and monies she received from her injury payout went into their first jointly purchased property. Sophie was unlucky to be involved in a second motor vehicle accident and received a further workplace payment; as a result, she spent a number of years away from the workforce.

Sophie's husband had no assets at the commencement of the relationship and accumulated business debt during the relationship. The couple ultimately purchased their matrimonial property, which was registered solely in the husband's name. By that stage, Sophie was not kept privy to any changes to the couple's financial situation and could not explain to me why the matrimonial property was not in both of their names.

Sophie and her husband attempted to conceive their first child for six years and underwent IVF treatment, which affected her terribly due to the complications. Their second child was also born via IVF.

It was only after separating that Sophie discovered a caveat was registered on the family home by a debt collector due to debt accumulated by her husband. The business debt that he had accumulated, and other hidden bills, began to surface at that time. At one point during the relationship, she had found thirty unopened envelopes hidden in the husband's car.

He had been failing to pay the liabilities of the business. Sophie's husband physically assaulted her when she confronted him about all of this debt. From that point on, he would lock the letterbox and tell Sophie she was not allowed to access it. Sophie reported constant family violence during the relationship, including physical and sexual assault.

Unbeknown to Sophie, in addition to monies owing pursuant to the caveat, there were also unpaid council rates, water rates and some $8,000 in electricity bills, resulting in further accumulated matrimonial debt. Sophie also discovered that monies in a bank account in her name (of at least $10,000) had been redrawn by her husband without her knowledge. Her husband had also been pawning her jewellery to pay for bills that he had accumulated.

After the separation, Sophie and her husband attempted to negotiate arrangements for the children. This involved her husband visiting the family home sporadically while she was present. It was difficult to negotiate agreed times and she found her husband to be unpredictable and unreliable.

His behaviour was intimidating. He would bang loudly on the front door to demand entry and he would yell and scream at her in front of the children. She ultimately stopped allowing the visits when one of the children reported that her husband had assaulted them by hitting them on the face during a visit. She had received advice from the police to cease the husband's time with the children at this point. Sophie experienced continued harassment from her husband. She ultimately blocked his telephone calls.

When the power was cut from the matrimonial property, Sophie moved in with her parents. She was there for four weeks while getting her finances in order. During that time, her husband returned to the matrimonial property and refused to vacate. It took significant negotiations with family members for the husband to allow Sophie and the children to return.

Upon Sophie's return, it was evident that her husband had taken most of her possessions and he had placed her wedding band on the kitchen bench. She was left without food, nappies and other essentials for the children, as the husband had removed them all. She was also left without basic items such as a refrigerator, vacuum cleaner, toaster or a kettle.

Sophie's husband had also strategically placed her deceased pet dog's medication in the middle of the cupboard for her to see. Sophie's beloved pet dog had died from a medical condition and her husband had deliberately failed to provide the pet its prescribed medication while Sophie was in hospital.

Sophie was not only experiencing the breakdown of a relationship and the trauma of family violence, but was now in a position of dire financial hardship. She had no option but to initiate court proceedings, seeking urgent orders for property settlement.

At the time of initiating those proceedings, her husband had not seen the children at all for nine months. Unfortunately for Sophie, he responded to the court proceedings by seeking parenting orders. The court ultimately ordered that the children spend supervised time with him every fortnight. During these sessions, the children refused to see their father, typically screaming and running to the supervisors for support.

Sophie, her husband and their children were all ordered to engage in a family report process, whereby they all met with an independent psychologist who had access to all of the court material, made their own independent enquiries (such as with the children's schools), observed interaction between the children and their parents, and ultimately wrote a report with recommendations to the judge.

The judge ultimately ordered that Sophie's husband and the children engage in reunification therapy with a clinical psychologist. The husband had not spent time with the children for two years at the time the clinical psychologist provided their reunification report to the court. Their view was that the children did not have the emotional capacity to manage reunification therapy and, therefore, they did not proceed with it.

After two and a half years in the court system, the final orders (as agreed by both parties) provided for Sophie to have full care of the children, for them to continue with their therapeutic counselling, and for the children to see a particular psychologist every six months so as to determine whether they were ready and willing to have a relationship with their father. The children's father is at liberty to send the psychologist gifts and cards to pass on to the children.

Those final orders were made over three years ago. According to Sophie, the children are still not ready to have a relationship with their father. It took tremendous bravery for Sophie to share her story and contribute her thoughts (shared later in this book), and I sincerely thank her for that bravery.

DAN'S STORY

Dan is a professional consultant who works in the corporate world. He was in a relationship with his ex-wife for some ten years and they have a young son together. His life was essentially turned upside down post separation when his ex-wife unilaterally took their son from a capital city in the eastern states to live in a country town in another state. Dan was in hospital, having surgery, when his son was relocated without his permission.

At the time, there were false allegations made against Dan, which were investigated by the Department of Family and Community Services. Those false allegations meant that Dan did not pursue a recovery order for his son to be immediately returned. So, in addition to having false allegations made against him, the logistics and expense of his son being relocated meant that he was not able to spend extensive time with him. Ultimately, Dan was not able to see his son for that period.

Dan soon relocated his life to the small country town to be close to his son. His consultancy business took a huge financial hit and he now feels essentially trapped in a town that he did not choose to live in.

The court proceedings were ongoing for approximately two years.

Dan's son has speech, cognitive and gross and fine motor skill delays, and is under the care of an NDIS (National Disability Insurance Scheme) plan. Dan and his ex-wife are required to maintain communication to discuss the needs of their son.

Throughout the court proceedings, Dan consistently said that he wanted to be able to co-parent with his ex-wife, particularly given their son's special needs. Unfortunately, Dan's ex-wife maintained that she wanted sole parental responsibility of their son and to exclude Dan from any decision making.

Ultimately, Dan and his ex-wife were able to agree on final orders that provide for their son to live with them for equal time on a 'week about' arrangement. As you can imagine, the issues that have arisen from Dan's experience, and his sense of loss, are complex.

JILLIAN'S STORY

Jillian came to me in her late fifties, having been in a relationship with her husband for some twenty years. Children from the relationship were now adults.

Jillian needed urgent assistance with her matrimonial property settlement. Despite Jillian and her husband having been separated for some ten years at that point, her ex-husband had put her home on the market without her knowledge or consent.

She had been living in a rural cottage at the back of the matrimonial property for all of that time, and her husband had always told her that she could remain living there. Jillian did not have a significant source of income to live elsewhere and loved her little cottage, which she'd spent countless hours renovating over the years.

The issue for Jillian, from a legal perspective, was that her urgent filing of the court proceedings was out of time. There were very complex legal issues, which did not seem at all fair to Jillian or to her family and friends. I will not go into detail around the specific legalities. However, you can imagine the sense of loss that Jillian experienced – not just around the breakdown of her marriage but also the ultimate loss of her home. She was unsuccessful in her application to the court and, as a result, suffered greatly from an emotional and financial perspective.

AMANDA'S STORY

Amanda was employed as a teacher at the time I was assisting her with her family law matter. Amanda and her ex-partner had been in a relationship for approximately ten years and had two children together. They separated when the youngest child was less than six months old.

Post separation, she said the communication between her and her ex-partner was poor. However, they attempted to make parenting arrangements themselves and also used a communication book. (A communication book is essentially a physical or electronic notebook, which allows parents to communicate with each other about children's needs. It may include things such as 'Johnny has a bit of a cold' or 'The assignment is due next Tuesday' or 'School camp is coming up – can you please pay half?') Amanda and her ex-partner were also able to resolve their property settlement by consent without going to court.

Attempts were made to mediate parenting matters via a community-based mediation service and then two lawyer-assisted conferences. Unfortunately for Amanda, her ex-partner then changed lawyers and instructed one of the 'big boy' law firms, which was quick to initiate court proceedings in relation to the children.

As part of the interview process for this book, Amanda shared with me her disbelief when she was served with court documents by a process server at her front door. She had never imagined that she would end up in court, disputing the arrangements for her children, and had no friends or family members who had knowledge of or experience with the process.

Amanda's ex-partner was pursuing final orders for the children to live with them equally on a 'week about' arrangement, which seemed unreasonable given the limited extended time her ex-partner had spent with the children, their different parenting styles, and the very poor communication between them.

She found herself dragged through litigious court proceedings, which took some eighteen months to finalise. The final orders were very much in line with the agreement we had promoted at the mediation process two years prior.

SUMMARY

That brings us to the end of chapter one. In the next chapter, we'll explore in more detail the notion of grief as an emotional response to a loss. I will discuss the different forms of grief and loss in the context of family law and separation. But first, here's a summary of the key points discussed in chapter one:

> You are not alone on your separation journey.

> While reading through the stories in this chapter, some of them may have really resonated with you. There were likely other stories that were entirely different to your separation journey. The important thing to remember is that everyone's story, including yours, is unique.

> Despite everyone's separation journey being unique, you will find that there are similarities in terms of the types of feelings that you are experiencing and also around your sense of loss.

CHAPTER TWO

UNDERSTANDING LOSS AND GRIEF IN A FAMILY LAW CONTEXT

As stated in the introduction, this book is written from a family law perspective. It's also based on my personal experience with grief, having experienced the deaths of both of my parents in a short space of time.

When we think of grief, we usually think of it in the context of death. The reality is that grief can occur as a result of various forms of loss. Remember, grief is the emotional response to a loss. Both death and separation are a crisis, and both can be traumatic in their own ways. Both can be a serious form of loss.

Over the past two years, I have immersed myself in books and other material on the topic of grief to help me understand my personal feelings of loss and grief. Reading about the theory of grief and loss, and reading about the experiences of others, has been life-changing for me. I hope it will be for you, too.

THE ORIGINAL THEORY ON GRIEF

The original theory around grief is linked to Elisabeth Kübler-Ross and her work in the book *On Death and Dying*, which was first published in 1969. She was a Swiss American psychiatrist who conducted pioneer studies on terminally ill patients.

During these studies, Elisabeth discovered the theory of the five stages of grief. This theory was originally developed to explain the stages that a terminally ill person goes through when facing their imminent death. Elisabeth later confirmed that these stages were also experienced by those who were suffering from grief (such as family members of the dying person).

The five stages are:

1. Denial
2. Anger
3. Bargaining
4. Depression
5. Acceptance

(We'll explore each of these stages, plus one more, in more detail in chapter three.)

Later in her career, Elisabeth said that the five stages are not chronological or linear. It was never her intention to 'package' everything neatly into five stages, and she regretted presenting it this way, as it caused confusion. Indeed, not everybody goes through every single stage, nor does anyone necessarily go through the stages in any particular order.

By listing stages of grief, there is the risk that people will try to fit themselves into each defined category. There is also the risk that you may feel as though you are meant to 'go through' or 'get through' the stages in order one to five. You do not need to 'tick off' or even relate to all of the stages, but it will help you through your journey to at least be aware of them.

And if you think the theory only applies to those grieving the death of a loved one, think again. It's also applicable to those dealing with the loss and breakdown of a relationship. In 1974, Elisabeth wrote *Questions and Answers on Death and Dying*, in which she confirmed (my emphasis added):

> *'A loss of <u>any kind</u> will provoke the same kind of adjustment reactions that we call "the stages of dying."'*

FORMS OF LOSS IN THE CONTEXT OF FAMILY LAW

In the context of family law, there are many types of loss that you may be experiencing. These include:

- The loss of your family
- The loss of your spouse/partner
- The loss of a child
- The loss of identity
- A financial loss
- The loss of your family home
- The loss of the 'future family'
- The loss of extended family relationships

An explanation around the loss of your family is fairly obvious. Whatever your family unit looked like prior to separation, that has been broken and no longer exists.

The loss of your spouse or partner also extends to the loss of love that you once experienced in that relationship.

The loss of a child may refer to the fact that you no longer live with them on a full-time basis, or even that you no longer see them at all. Pete Nicholls, the CEO of Parents Beyond Breakup, is strongly in agreeance that the men he assists have suffered loss in the form of grief:

> 'A common theme is that of dads describing the loss of contact with their child(ren) as a living bereavement. In some ways [it is] worse than the real thing because there is no absolute finality to it, and only ongoing agony and lack of knowing if you'll see them again, when that might happen and if, by the time you do, they'll remember or even love you by then. It is like torture that won't stop.'

Family consultant Artemicia Nisyrios believes there are multiple aspects of grief and loss following the breakdown of a relationship:

> 'Not only the loss of a partner and the fantasy of what that partnership could have brought them... It may also be the loss of their identity as a wife or husband.
>
> '... They may grieve the loss of access to their children on a daily basis, loss of contact with extended family

members, and other social networks created within that partnership. They may also grieve their sense of control and power that was sustained by the relationship.

'Often clients grieve other significant losses such as their family home, pets, cars, photo albums and so on. Some may also lose their employment as they need to relocate to safety or take time off to care for themselves or their children.'

Financial loss may include the financial pressure of no longer being in a two-income family unit or no longer having the sole financial provider in your life supporting you. There may be immediate loss of finances, or concerns about how you will financially support yourself moving forward. You may be concerned that you will suffer the loss of your family home because you cannot afford to stay there. You may be concerned that you will suffer a financial loss by having to pay out settlement monies to your ex-partner.

The loss of a 'future family' may mean the loss of what the future was to hold for you. You may have lost your hopes, dreams and expectations for the future. Nobody goes into a relationship thinking that it will *not* be successful. Nobody plans to have children with someone, or build a financial future together, if they know the relationship will ultimately break down.

These are just a few examples of the loss you may be experiencing. When you really think about your own situation and the way it makes you feel, you will likely relate to at least one of these examples. You are likely to also have examples or experiences in loss that are very specific to you.

YOUR LOSS IS SIGNIFICANT

Loss in a family law context must be recognised as a significant loss. Although nobody has died, there are still strong and often conflicting emotions that come along with it.

Separation and divorce is the death of a relationship, along with the hopes and dreams and expectations that are attached to that. So, again, it is perfectly normal to feel a sense of grief because you have experienced a major loss.

According to Beyond Blue, which provides information and support in relation to mental health, grief can feel all-encompassing:

> 'Grief is expressed in many ways and it can affect every part of your life; your emotions, thoughts and behaviour, beliefs, physical health, your sense of self and identity, and your relationships with others. Grief can leave you feeling sad, angry, anxious, shocked, regretful, relieved, overwhelmed, isolated, irritable or numb.'

Another excellent resource on grief is Megan Devine's book, *It's OK That You're Not OK: Meeting Grief and Loss in a Culture That Doesn't Understand*. Megan's summary of grief can certainly apply to people who have experienced a loss due to separation and family law issues:

> 'Grief is a part of love. Grief is love for others. Grief is an extension of love ... And love is really hard. Excruciating at times.'

Please take a moment to re-read those words as they are so important. As part of your separation journey, it is important to pause and acknowledge that grief is a part of love, and to also acknowledge that you have indeed suffered a loss in the breakdown of your relationship.

SUMMARY

That brings us to the end of chapter two. In the next chapter, we will delve a little deeper into the various stages of grief, and how they relate to you and your separation. But first, here's a summary of the key points discussed in chapter two:

> Grief can occur as a result of various forms of loss, including the breakdown of a relationship. Your loss in the family law context must be recognised as a significant loss.

> Your grief is an emotional response to the loss that you have experienced.

> You do not need to fit yourself into the stages of grief. Remember that this is not a box-ticking exercise. You may relate to some or all of the stages, and you may experience them in a non-linear way.

CHAPTER THREE

THE 5 STAGES OF GRIEF, PLUS 1 MORE

As discussed in chapter two, Elisabeth Kübler-Ross made it clear that there is no absolute or 'universal' theory on grief. No two reactions will be exactly the same. One of the reasons for this is that everyone's sense of loss is unique, based on their particular situation.

Elisabeth also said that there is no correct way to grieve. Your experience of loss – and the subsequent grief you will feel – will differ to someone else's experience. Your separation and family law journey will also differ from others'. However, there are also some similarities, which link back to the various stages of grief.

Remember, the stages in Elisabeth's theory are:

1. Denial
2. Anger
3. Bargaining
4. Depression
5. Acceptance

In this chapter, we'll look at each of these stages in more detail. But first, I'd like to discuss another stage of grief.

ANTICIPATORY GRIEF

In addition to the five stages of grief as outlined by Elisabeth Kübler-Ross, another stage of grief that you may be experiencing is anticipatory grief. As a family lawyer, I often meet with clients who have not yet made the decision to leave a relationship but are wanting to obtain some advice around what their options are if they were to separate.

It is a smart idea to get an overview of both parenting and property matters prior to separation, and to protect your position as best as possible in the event that you do ultimately decide to separate. Others are in the process of relationship counselling but know that, in reality, there is no saving the relationship. They may also already be experiencing a sense of loss and also concern for what is likely to follow.

Anticipatory grief shows how we all move through the stages of loss at different times. If you are the person who has initiated the separation, then there is a good chance that you have already experienced some of the stages prior to separation and certainly prior to your ex-partner.

For example, my client Jane recalls trying to leave her husband prior to having their first child some eight years ago. They engaged in relationship counselling, even though she knew deep down that she wanted to end the relationship.

My client John said he realised that his relationship was over about a year before the actual separation, which he ultimately initiated. He stayed in the relationship longer than he really wanted to for the sake of his children and because he didn't want to lose his relationship with them.

Both Jane and John experienced anticipatory grief, albeit in different ways.

DENIAL

Denial is the first stage of grief as identified by Elisabeth Kübler-Ross. Denial is a form of defence that is used when we are not able to accept the facts or accept our reality. One form of denial experienced by those who have separated is thoughts along the lines of, 'How can this be happening to me?' There is some level of disbelief that your relationship has come to an end or that it has ended the way that it has.

An example of denial that I see quite frequently as a family lawyer are clients who 'lawyer shop'. Don't get me wrong. Before engaging a lawyer, you should definitely explore your options and perhaps meet with two to three lawyers before deciding on someone who is the right fit for you. You need to be comfortable with your lawyer and also confident in their abilities. A bit of empathy from your lawyer can also help!

The difficulty, however, is when clients are going from lawyer to lawyer (usually in a first consultation setting) to try to obtain the advice that they *want* to hear. It is not uncommon for me to see clients who have been to see other lawyers prior to our consultation, who have perhaps inaccurate or unrealistic expectations. This may be the client's interpretation of what has been said. Or the advice may have come from an inexperienced lawyer or a lawyer solely focused on fees. That said, it is not uncommon for the client to be in some form of denial around how their family law matter is likely to progress and the likely forms of settlement.

Unfortunately, there'll probably always be lawyers who are willing to tell you what you want to hear if you pay them. Please be aware of this. It is not a sign of denial to be careful in choosing your expert family lawyer. However, if you are shopping around until you find what you want to be told, then unfortunately this is denial of the situation and the likely outcome, and it is likely to lead to disappointment and potentially the loss of thousands of dollars.

It is for this reason that legal aid is both merit *and* means tested. The client has to have merit as to the orders sought (if there are proceedings) or in fact merit to initiate proceedings in the first instance. For example, if a mother has not seen her children for a number of years, it would be unfair (and unethical) of me to say that she will obtain full custody of her children. I refuse to do so.

I have been employed by Legal Aid in different states as both a duty lawyer at court and also in the area of general advice. During that time, I would see clients come back more than once, hoping to see a different lawyer, presumably to obtain different advice.

Sometimes, your denial or lawyer shopping can come about after listening to 'advice' from well-meaning friends and family members. Your friends and family should be able to support you during this time, but should not give you family law advice. Listening to their stories or their friends' stories (even worse!) can lead to confusion about specific advice for your specific matter and, as a result, can lead to denial of the situation that you actually find yourself in.

Another form of denial is putting your head in the sand. I see it all too often, whereby I will write to the other party on behalf of my client with a view to negotiating property and/or parenting matters amicably. Unfortunately, it is not uncommon for that correspondence to be ignored as the recipient is finding it too difficult to deal with at that time. The follow-up correspondence is also ignored. Unfortunately, this often forces my client to initiate court proceedings, which is very disappointing for everyone.

I have seen the denial continue throughout the court process in that the respondent will fail to attend court and/or fail to file responding documents. This level of denial can be very dangerous in that it can lead to ex parte orders being made in their absence. In other words, the court has jurisdiction to make parenting and property orders in the absence of a party. These extreme orders may range from a final order for 'no time' with the children through to an order for the matrimonial property in the sole name of the non-engaging party to be sold. I have experienced both of those types of orders. In the second instance, the court even had the jurisdiction to sign transfer documents for the sale of a property. In short, if you are at this level of denial, you are in trouble.

According to Pete Nicholls, both shock and denial are common reactions for men in the wake of a separation. In fact, they're often the first response.

Based on his many conversations with the men he helps, Pete said a common pattern of separation is that the female grieves the relationship breakdown many months prior to the actual separation. When the couple does eventually separate, the female may actually experience a sense of relief, whereas, for the male, *'it is often the exact opposite and the separation (sometimes out of the blue) is where it starts. At the very point she often wants to be left alone, he needs to talk more than ever. It's a mess. It feels unreal to those who did not see it coming.'*

In the case of one of my clients, her husband disputed the divorce application and would not agree to the divorce order being made. He was adamant that the relationship was not over, despite the length of separation (at least twelve months, as required by law) and the fact that his wife had engaged a lawyer.

There are so many examples where one party at separation is in denial and holds hope of reconciliation. Amanda, who shared her story in chapter one, said that in the wake of her separation, her ex-partner refused to leave the family home and slept on the couch for months. He was not in a position to take over the family home, as he would not have been able to meet the mortgage repayments. I suspect that people in this situation are, to a certain extent, in a position of denial and certainly in a position of uncertainty as to what their future may hold. I can appreciate the difficulty he would have had in ultimately leaving the family home and his children.

You may not be in the denial stage, but your ex-partner may be. It is important to understand this stage so as to better communicate and negotiate any unresolved issues. For someone experiencing denial, not much is making sense for them. They may not be able to fathom what went wrong in the relationship and why there is no possibility of reconciliation. Everything may seem overwhelming for them at this point in time. Your ex-partner is likely to be experiencing many of the same stressors as you and feeling grief themselves. Having some level of understanding and empathy around where their thinking is at will assist in your communication with them.

ANGER

The second stage of grief, as outlined by Elisabeth Kübler-Ross, is anger. I've read that it is *not* uncommon during separation and divorce to not experience this stage of grief. But based on my experience, and the clients that I have interacted with, I struggle to think of anyone who did not experience some element of anger at some point during their grieving process.

Artemicia Nisyrios believes anger is often caused by an inability to make sense of your emotions. She says it can also be a form of protection:

> *'I think sometimes anger is an easier emotion to express and can be protective, because while you remain angry you are more immune to looking inward and feeling a true sense of sadness. Sadness at not only the loss*

of [the] relationship but also your loss of identity connected to that relationship.'

Anger is a way of masking pain; the pain you feel is essentially withheld underneath the anger. Anger is a response to a sense of injustice. It is a normal and healthy response, and not something that you should try and suppress. In fact, anger is a helpful part of the grieving process in that it helps you to *heal* because holding onto anger, and not having an outlet to express your anger, can be self-destructive. The key is having a safe outlet to express your anger. We'll touch on this more later. But first, I want to share a bit about my own feelings of anger.

Having experienced grief through the death of my parents, I definitely experienced anger… at its finest! I displayed a certain level of anger towards many medical staff and government departments. At one point, I punched a wall at a hospital (it felt good in the moment, but my hand was very sore for at least a week afterwards!). I hung up the phone on a 'useless' doctor. Yes, I was angry!

Looking back now, I realise that what I was actually feeling was confusion and frustration (at a medical system which was not meeting the needs of my dying parents), powerlessness and stress. This manifested as anger.

Likewise, our family law system has so many flaws and so many opportunities for you to feel angry… and often for good reason! (This is in addition to the anger you may feel as part of your grief process.) I am reminded of my experiences with clients who have behaved angrily or poorly throughout the family law process. I understand that you may be feeling a whole range of emotions, including anger. However, be careful how you express that anger. Most lawyers have a mental list of badly behaved clients. It is generally not in your interest to be on that list!

I'm not just referring to how you deal with your legal team, but how you behave in court. This is potentially the worst place to be displaying your anger! I tell clients to keep a poker face in the courtroom, as things will be said that they disagree with and that are downright offensive sometimes.

If you are unfortunate enough to be in court, or if it looks like you will be going to court, also keep in mind that you don't want to express your anger or aggression towards the Independent Children's Lawyer (if appointed). I have acted in hundreds of matters as a children's lawyer and I do remember the matters where someone was rude to me. I remember very well one party refusing to shake my hand and telling me that he did not want me involved in the proceedings! I tried to explain that the court had appointed a lawyer to act for the children and that my presence was not really optional.

Showing anger towards your ex-partner should also be avoided, although I understand this is easier said than done. It is not uncommon at the time of separation for there to be irrational behaviour or even situational violence. Sometimes, the separation can come as a surprise for you. At other times, children have been removed without your consent. Money may be secretly drawn from bank accounts. Perhaps you feel like your ex-partner is making the property and/or children's negotiations more protracted than they need to be. Or you may feel you have been taken to court unnecessarily. These are all examples of where anger may be present – and often for good reason.

Showing anger towards your ex-partner goes beyond face-to-face communication, too. You may get angry at them via text messages or Facebook Messenger or other forms of social media. Please remember that if your matter does end up in court, these angry messages may find themselves annexed to an affidavit (a sworn statement in which each party tells their 'story' and sets out their concerns), which will not be helpful for you.

Angry communication in itself may also make an otherwise workable matter deteriorate to the point where there can be no positive communication and your matter ends up in court. It is also not helpful moving forward, particularly if you have children together and need to communicate with your ex-partner for many years to come.

If you do have children, remember to be mindful of the communication that you have with your ex-partner in their presence. If you are experiencing anger, then it is all too easy to behave badly at handover or when speaking on the phone. Try to remain child-focused and keep your cool, no matter the reason for the separation or how angry you are.

Pete Nicholls says anger is a common reaction to a relationship breakdown and loss, but that it is also a response to a sense of hopelessness. He regards it as *'a normal reaction to an abnormal situation'*. What is critical is the way that the anger is managed or channelled.

His support groups are able to provide men (and women) with a forum to express their anger in a safe environment, away from others, without being intimidated or judged. Pete is of the view that it is very important for men in particular to have that safe forum to be able to express their anger, rather than refusing any displays of anger whatsoever, which is the approach taken by some other support services. One of the men engaged in the Dads in Distress support group summed it up this way:

> 'With no good way to externalise our pain, is it really any wonder some dads turn to violence, against themselves or others?'

Roxanne Nathan also recognises the importance of being able to feel anger:

> 'I am of the opinion that all emotions are useful and should be experienced and integrated in order to move forward towards wellbeing. We are coming out of a period in time in history where men particularly were told to be stoic and not show emotion, that showing emotion was a weakness, and where women's emotions were considered as something not to be taken seriously.
>
> 'We should as therapeutic practitioners encourage emotions to be experienced, [as] this helps with the healing process of grief and loss. My key phrase to clients is, "It's okay to feel any emotions, but it's what you do with that feeling that matters." A typical example is that it is okay to be angry with your ex-partner, but it is not okay to hit, harm or threaten them.'

As you move forward on your journey, anger is likely to stay with you and rear its head from time to time – not only as a direct consequence of loss but also if you feel direct anger towards your ex-partner due to their conduct and behaviour. My client Sophie separated from her ex-husband some years ago. However, she still feels anger towards him and doesn't feel as though time has lessened the anger:

> *'It's not the kind of anger that festers or is consuming but I do find myself triggered occasionally and I'm reminded of the damage he caused. Whether it be the endless struggle to financially cope, or the trust issues that have prevented me from loving someone else again. I have made complete peace with the cessation of our marriage. However, my experience was incredibly damaging and he is a dangerous individual, capable of immense destruction, damage and hurt. No amount of therapy has lessened my conviction.'*

As for me, I'm pleased to report that I am no longer in the angry stage of grief. I now have more clarity, which is largely due to some of the tools that I will discuss later in this book and also from having a better understanding of the stages of grief, which I was not aware of previously. Like Sophie, I still do get angry from time to time, and it usually comes on unexpectedly, but being able to understand *why* I am feeling that way (because of grief) can help me to rein it in and better manage it.

BARGAINING

Bargaining is the third stage of grief in Elisabeth Kübler-Ross's theory. I suspect that within a family law context, bargaining often goes alongside denial. In the section on denial, I spoke about people who were not willing to accept the separation and were in denial in that respect. The bargaining stage can go one step further in that people are trying to use bargaining as a tool to repair the relationship.

Bargaining can be an attempt to rebuild a relationship. It is often a last-ditch effort to ensure the separation does not take place. Often, it is done with promises or even threats. It may be that one party is willing to do anything to make the relationship 'right'. They promise to change or go to therapy to fix any problems. They are not willing to accept the end of the relationship – hence, the bargaining.

The types of thoughts around bargaining are 'If only...' and 'What if I did things differently?' One party may insist on relationship counselling to ensure that the relationship doesn't end. At times, the person who has not ended the relationship may approach mutual friends and family members in a bid to get them onside so as to convince the other person not to separate.

One of my clients described the difficulty that she had with her husband drinking alcohol to excess for many years prior to separation. Attempts were made to meet with a family therapist, with recommendations that he obtain a mental health care plan and/or engage with a psychologist or service to assist with his alcohol addiction.

Over the years, my client repeatedly told her husband that she would leave the relationship unless he obtained that help. He never did get assistance, and it was only when she finally left the matrimonial property with the children that concrete promises were made by him to obtain the help he needed.

Bargaining can also be prevalent in matters where there is family violence, in terms of promises to 'change' and that the violent behaviour will stop. I have seen this hundreds of times over the years while assisting victims of family violence. At times, the client will give the relationship another shot. However, if they have finally reached the point of obtaining legal advice, then it is more likely to be a case of 'too little too late'. Unfortunately, it is not uncommon to see people in this stage make threats to or about their ex-partner, their family and/or their children in an attempt to keep the relationship intact.

Be mindful that when someone is in the bargaining stage, they are not likely to be thinking clearly, are struggling to find meaning, and will do anything possible to repair the relationship. It can be extremely difficult to negotiate during this stage.

It is often at this point where I see a client who will give instructions such as, 'I don't care, he can have all the assets, I will just walk away.' I also hear clients saying things such as, 'She can have the children,' even in circumstances where it may not be appropriate, because the client is still in the stages of denial and bargaining.

It is usually at this point that clients are trying to fix a perceived wrong (such as cheating on their ex-partner) or generally are still in the bargaining stage of attempting to repair their relationship.

It is very difficult for a family lawyer in these circumstances to act for clients while trying to protect their financial interest or to protect their parenting arrangements.

If a client has instructed me to put forward a proposal that I think is unreasonable and not in their best interest, then I will encourage them to take a little extra time to consider the options. I'll also put my concerns in writing and have them sign a letter of advice to confirm that they understand that advice. There are, of course, other reasons why someone may be providing instructions that are not in their best interest. Perhaps they are exhausted and are struggling generally with the jurisdiction and/or separation.

DEPRESSION

The fourth stage of loss, as outlined by Elisabeth Kübler-Ross, is depression. Separation and divorce are often compared to a traumatic event such as death. Rates of depression for those going through separation and/or the family law system are high, and life events such as separation can trigger depression. Even among the broader population, the statistics are concerning.

According to Beyond Blue, three million Australians are living with depression or anxiety. Those suffering depression are at much higher risk of suicide, particularly men. In Australia each day, six out of every eight suicides are male suicides. Alarmingly, the number of men who die by suicide each year in Australia is double that of the national road toll.

This is what Beyond Blue has to say about grief and depression:

> *'Grief and depression are quite different but they can appear similar as they can both lead to feelings of intense sadness, insomnia, poor appetite and weight loss. Depression stands out from grief as being more persistent, with constant feelings of emptiness and despair and a difficulty feeling pleasure or joy. If you notice that depression symptoms continue, or your grief begins to get in the way of how you live, work, share relationships or live day-to-day, then it's important to get support or professional help.'*

In the context of a separation, depression sometimes occurs when the reality of your situation has set in (such as when you have moved past the bargaining stage). This stage of depression is an appropriate response to a loss and is not necessarily a sign of mental illness.

My client John discussed the loss he felt when he moved out of the family home. It was not so much the loss of the relationship with his ex-partner, but the loss of not seeing his children every day. He described feeling *'terrible not seeing my children. The quietness was very hard to deal with, without the noise of children in the house. I found this very depressing and sad.'*

If you have experienced depression as a result of your relationship loss, then you are likely to feel trapped in the past (as opposed to feeling worried and anxious about the future).

The feelings that you may experience during the depression

stage are not always just feelings of sadness or feeling 'low'. It goes deeper than that. If you are suffering from depression as a grief response, then the feelings may be incredibly intense and protracted. During this stage, you can become very withdrawn from life and wonder what the point of everything is. As Elisabeth Kübler-Ross said in her 2005 book, *On Grief and Grieving: Finding the Meaning of Grief Through the Five Stages of Loss:*

> *'Life feels pointless. To get out of bed may as well be climbing a mountain. You feel heavy, and being upright takes something from you that you just don't have to give. If you find a way to get through your daily activities, each of them seems as empty and pointless as the last one.'*

Things can completely slow down during this process. Elisabeth goes on to explain that if grief is a part of the healing process, then depression is one of the necessary steps along the journey:

> *'When you allow yourself to experience depression, it will leave as soon as it has served its purpose in your loss.'*

Most of my clients have described feeling depressed post separation and/or have been prescribed antidepressants. My informal observation over almost twenty years is that there seems to be an increase in the number of people going through separation who are reliant on antidepressants. Remember that your feelings during this stage of depression are a natural response to loss. Antidepressants may be useful if a 'normal' depression becomes clinical. In some cases, you may need more management, including psychotherapy. However, you should seek your own independent medical advice.

On this topic, Peter Nicholls highlights the importance of understanding situational depression. He reports that most of the men he sees fall into this category and that they are able to find solutions through regular peer support.

He says, *'I'd argue that what people tend to talk about as depression is often misdiagnosed for separating men. It's more a case of hopelessness, and a lack of wanting to go on when that becomes your belief. It is not chemical in nature but can be altered chemically; if done so though, it rarely achieves much other than to dull the individual down even further until the prompting situation is addressed.'*

While Pete's comments are specifically in relation to men, it's fair to say that women may also feel a sense of hopelessness following their separation. If you are in this stage of depression, then you may find that you are having difficulty functioning at this time. This can cause all sorts of problems, especially if you are in a family law dispute, have children who need taking care of or have employment commitments.

During this stage, you're also more likely to make bad decisions and take risks because you simply do not care about the ramifications. You may do silly things that impact your family law matter, such as making irrational financial decisions, withholding your children from their other parent, or even showing a disregard for court orders. I've also seen people fail to engage in court proceedings because it is just too difficult for them.

THE 5 STAGES OF GRIEF, PLUS 1 MORE

In his bestseller *The Subtle Art of Not Giving a F*ck*, Mark Manson talks about people being self-absorbed and how it is not uncommon to think that we are the only one suffering injustices. When you are in the depression stage of grief, it is not uncommon to behave in a way that is self-absorbed. You could be so self-absorbed with your own worries that you don't notice other things taking place around you, or other problems that other people may have.

As a practising family lawyer, I have to remind myself that despite all of the things I may be going through (including my own grief), the stories I hear from clients and the concerns that they have are the most important thing in *their* world at that moment. Those issues that may seem minor or not overly important to me are front and centre for someone else. It is all too easy to take the viewpoint that you should take responsibility for your loss and stop being a victim of your loss. Unfortunately, there will be people who hold this viewpoint and, no doubt, you have experienced that.

If you yourself are currently self-absorbed, then you may not even realise it at this stage. If you re-read this book at a later date, it may be that you are able to reflect and acknowledge that perhaps you were, to a certain extent, in this mindset. The other thing to keep in mind is that if your ex-partner has a victim mindset, then you are unlikely to have any control over that. However, being mindful of the reasons for their mindset and feelings of self-absorption may help you to understand them better and assist with any ongoing communication with them.

One final point before we move on. It's not my intention to

trivialise or to generalise mental health issues and depression to such an extent as to cause offence. Mental health is a very complex issue. Depression due to loss is also very complex, particularly when there are other underlying mental health issues. At the end of this book, you'll find a number of professional resources and referrals that may be helpful for you or your loved ones in this regard.

ACCEPTANCE

The fifth and final stage of loss, as outlined by Elisabeth Kübler-Ross, is acceptance. Please do not mistake acceptance as moving into a 'happy stage'. As Elisabeth says, *'Finding acceptance may be just having more good days than bad.'*

Accepting the situation and your reality does not mean that you are okay with what has happened. It is about accepting what you have gone though, that your relationship is over (and anything else in terms of loss that flows from that) and that the situation will not change. In other words, you accept your new reality.

In the words of Eleanor Roosevelt, *'You have to accept whatever comes and the only important thing is that you meet it with courage and with the best that you have to give.'*

The acceptance phase is, of course, very different to both the denial and bargaining stages of grief. It may take considerable time. But when you have reached the stage of acceptance, it means you have learned to live with your loss and, more importantly, have learned to live in what is *your* new normal.

THE 5 STAGES OF GRIEF, PLUS 1 MORE

I commonly see clients re-partnering quite quickly post separation. You may have re-partnered or you may be surprised and upset at how quickly your ex-partner has re-partnered. Entering into a new relationship is not necessarily an acceptance in relation to your grief and loss (although it may be).

Sometimes, it may be that you or your ex-partner has re-partnered without having fully accepted that the previous relationship is over. It can, at times, be a coping mechanism and in some way a denial in relation to the loss of the previous relationship. At other times, you may have fully accepted that your previous relationship is over and have comfortably moved on with a new partner.

Unfortunately, in my experience, when I observe one party having moved on 'quickly', it can cause a breakdown in communication and can take the parties a step backwards in terms of their ongoing communication.

One of the difficulties with relationship breakdowns and trying to resolve your family law matter is that it can be protracted. Every letter received from a law firm, every SMS from your partner, every email sent to your ex-partner, every discussion with your accountant or conveyancer and every court hearing can be incredibly draining. Acceptance is not an 'end point' but rather a process that you will experience. You may feel that you have reached a level of acceptance, but that it is soon lost given the nature of family law matters.

On the flip side, you may find that when you reach this stage, your decision making is clear and you are in a better headspace in terms of being able to communicate with your ex-partner and/or negotiate your family law matter. You may be relieved that you didn't make those all-important decisions when you were experiencing denial or bargaining! Acceptance will look different to every reader of this book.

SUMMARY

That brings us to the end of chapter three. In the next chapter, we will delve deeper into the different types of support that you can and should have in place to help you navigate this difficult period of loss. But first, here's a summary of the key points discussed in chapter three:

> The stages of grief and loss that you may be experiencing, or that your ex-partner may be experiencing, can include anticipatory grief, denial, anger, bargaining, depression and acceptance.

> There is no correct way to grieve and no two responses will be exactly the same.

> Remember that professional resources and referrals have been provided for you at the end of this book. These are designed to help you through the grieving process.

CHAPTER FOUR
───────────

GETTING THE RIGHT SUPPORT

Dealing with the breakdown of your relationship is likely to be one of the most traumatic times in your life. It is for that reason that you need to build a good support team around you.

In addition to friends and family members (which we'll discuss later in the chapter), your support team should include a number of key professionals. This will help to ensure that you are best placed to deal with your separation from both a legal and personal safety perspective. Your professional support team may include the following:

- Lawyer – family law
- Lawyer – criminal law (I'll explain when this might be necessary)
- Barrister
- Men's and women's support groups
- Domestic and family violence support groups

The various members of your professional support team will each have different skills and strengths. But when it comes to building that team, perhaps you don't know where to start. In this chapter, my aim is to shed some light on the work of these professionals and support groups, and outline how they can help you. Let's start with the one I'm most familiar with – my own profession as a family lawyer.

THE FAMILY LAWYER

I find that for many clients who initially consult with me, it is their first time speaking with a lawyer. Others have already telephoned legal aid services, government family law advice lines or community legal services.

All of those services can be a good starting point. However, they are generally limited in the legal advice that they are able to provide. I really enjoy speaking with a client for the first time and advising them of their legal options, and how best to proceed. It is not uncommon for this conversation to be a massive relief for the client; it can even be empowering in the sense of regaining a sense of control.

I recommend that you do not consult with a generalist law firm that 'dabbles' in the family law jurisdiction, but rather consult with a specialist family lawyer. A generalist law firm may seem like a cheaper option. However, the advantage of being in the family law system, via a family lawyer, is that the jurisdiction is national (with some exceptions in Western Australia), so there are no restrictions based on where you live. Also, a generalist firm is likely to be slower to complete work, not across the issues, not well respected in the jurisdiction, and not likely to put you in the best possible legal position.

Likewise, take caution if instructing a junior lawyer. I recall my first role as a new graduate; I was extremely 'green' and also did not have much guidance or support. I was shown my office, provided around sixty files, and off I went! I was very much a junior, but charging out similar rates to my senior colleagues. I was certainly learning in the role, which ultimately was a fantastic learning opportunity for me... but perhaps not the best experience for my clients! When I appear in court now, I have the advantage of being senior and I use that to my advantage wherever possible.

Many firms offer a first free meeting with potential new clients. One of the reasons for this is for both the firm and the client to make an assessment as to whether you are the right fit for each other. It is very important that when you instruct a lawyer, you are confident in their legal abilities but also comfortable with them. For this reason, I typically advise potential new clients to consult with another one or two solicitors by way of comparison. Engaging a lawyer is an important decision for you and it can also be costly. It is important that you instruct your lawyer on an informed basis.

It is not uncommon for clients to cry during or at the end of their free meeting with my family law firm. As I said earlier, this is often a sign of relief, as they know they will be guided through the process.

Do you feel that sense of relief when meeting with your potential lawyer? How are their people skills? How has your experience been with the firm so far? How were the reception staff or paralegals whom you spoke with prior to the meeting? How were you greeted when you arrived at the office for the first time? How did you feel at the office? Do you think you will be supported through the process?

Keep in mind that most first free interviews will only be around thirty minutes long. There is limited time to go into your matter in detail. It will, however, give you a good feel for the lawyer and their family law knowledge. At the end of the meeting, they should have a general idea of what your legal issues are, the various options available to you, and hopefully an indication of costs if you are to instruct them.

Ultimately, it will also depend on what you want from your lawyer. Do you want a lawyer who is aggressive (the so-called 'shark')? Do you want someone who will support you and shows empathy? Someone who is results-driven? If your communication with your ex-partner is amicable, then you should consider receiving initial advice from a collaborative law firm, which has specialist family lawyers to help both parties resolve their differences in the most amicable way. Another option may be a solicitor who will assist by running an informal conference with your ex-partner and their solicitor. That can also be a useful way to more quickly resolve your property and/or parenting matters.

Earlier in this book, I discussed clients behaving badly. This is a timely reminder not to get your lawyer offside. I had one client recently ring my personal mobile at 7am to relay something that she considered urgent. The early call was not appreciated.

That said, if you feel your lawyer is not responding to communication adequately, or you are not happy with their work (or lack thereof), then there is nothing wrong with asking for an explanation. If you do not understand something, then insist it is explained to you in layman's terms. I follow a number of forums on social media and always see comments from people who have lawyers but are asking the 'layperson community' for their opinions on their matter. Frankly, if you are taking these steps, then there should be concerns in terms of your representation. Perhaps you need to be asking your solicitor more questions, or asking them to clarify things when you don't understand. Remember, their role is to support you.

Just as you should not rely on laypeople for legal advice, you should not rely on your lawyer to be your emotional support person. As a family lawyer, I often feel like a social worker! Consider how much you would pay a counsellor or social worker per hour. I suspect it would be less than a lawyer's hourly rate. I find it important to show empathy to my clients, and I am certainly not going to stop them from confiding in me if they are upset or feel it is important for me to know how they're feeling.

However, while it is important to be honest and transparent with your lawyer, it's also important to remember that lawyers are not trained as mental health professionals, so they will not be best placed to provide you with that assistance. Your lawyer may be able to provide a valuable referral to a mental health professional. We'll discuss mental health in more detail in chapter seven.

THE CRIMINAL LAWYER

So, why might you need a criminal lawyer? If an Intervention Order has been taken out against you, or if you have been charged with any sort of assault charges by your ex-partner, then you should have them dealt with.

An Intervention Order will not in itself preclude you from spending time with your children. However, if there are any outstanding criminal charges, then your matter may not be deemed appropriate for mediation, which may mean that your avenue to resolve parenting issues is via court. The court may delay proceedings pending the outcome of criminal proceedings. Your family and criminal solicitor would work together in that situation to ensure that you are protected from both a criminal law and family law perspective.

THE BARRISTER

My firm does a lot of in-house court work, but from time to time we do brief external barristers. We generally recommend a barrister (who is a family law specialist, of course!) based on whom we think will be a suitable match for that client.

Often, I will help clients select a barrister based on their specific legal and advocacy knowledge as opposed to their people skills. This acts as a heads-up to the client that the barrister is very valuable (in terms of the service they provide) and there for a specific purpose. In other words, don't expect general chit-chat about your weekend!

Having the right barrister on your professional team can also be invaluable. We are now seeing barristers have more input in terms of providing opinions during the negotiation stage and also attending informal conferences. Having expert opinions at this stage may avoid protracted negotiation and/or litigation.

Be mindful that barristers will have their own agenda in terms of the information they need to extract from you. You may presume that they have read the entire brief and that you do not need to explain your whole story to them again, however, this is not always the case.

You are under no obligation to retain the same barrister. If you are unhappy with them, then you should speak with your solicitor to discuss alternative representation.

SUPPORT GROUPS

If you were referred to a family violence officer or support group either during or post separation, then you may want to consider linking back into that service for ongoing support. They will also be best placed to recommend alternative support services, courses and groups that are best for your particular circumstances.

There are also family court support services for women, whereby you can choose to have someone attend court with you. Your lawyer should also know how to book a safety room for you. This is a room at court where security will escort you to and from, and nobody is able to have access aside from you and your legal team.

It would be remiss of me not to mention the difficulties that men face during their separation and loss, particularly around the lack of specific service providers. I have already mentioned their overrepresentation in suicide rates in Australia. My view is that there does not appear to be the same level of support available to men that we see for women.

There has been a large injection of government funding to assist women and children who are victims of family violence. I fully support this and believe there is still a shortfall. I do feel, however, that men could be better served as well. At the end of this book, I have included the contact details for Parents Beyond Breakup, which has a particularly good support group for men (Dads in Distress).

FRIENDS AND FAMILY

Let me repeat what I wrote at the start of this chapter: **Dealing with the breakdown of your relationship is likely to be one of the most traumatic times in your life.** It is for that reason that you need to not only build a good professional team around you, but have good supports in place in general. Dealing with your loss, and also potentially the stress of family law negotiations or court on top of that, can seem overwhelming.

When your relationship breaks down, you may feel that you are initially receiving good support from well-meaning friends and family members. The truth is, however, that their world carries on and, at times, you may feel forgotten because the feelings that you are feeling remain the most important thing in *your* world. (We discussed this briefly in the previous chapter.) Many people think that the point of grief is to get through it or out of it as soon as you can. As a result, people can start to question you if you are not back to 'normal' or are taking time to work through your loss.

Have you found that friends and family members were a bit more supportive at the beginning, when you first confided in them that you were separating from your partner? Have you found that those messages of support and telephone calls have died off? It's not that your friends and family don't care about you, but they have their own lives to live. As time goes on, your loss can feel forgotten or people struggle to know how they can help.

My client Liarne describes how her family and friendship support dropped off over time, even saying, *'I think by the end of it they were all as over it as I was!'* My client Dan also reached out to his friends and family for advice and support but, as with most challenging times in life, only a handful of close friends provided ongoing care and concern for his welfare.

You may also find that there are perhaps well-meaning friends and family members who say things to you during your loss that you simply find offensive. I wonder if you have been on the receiving end of comments such as: 'You'll find another partner' or 'At least you get to see the kids' or 'We never liked him anyway.'

The way society is trained to think is to replace your loss or to fix your loss. When you are grieving or experiencing loss, people will try to stop you from feeling the way you do (by attempting to make you happy) or, alternatively, to replace what you have lost. Comments like 'She wasn't right for you' or 'You can do better than him' are common. These comments are not helpful and may only make you feel worse.

Another comment people tend to make in relation to your loss is: 'I know how you feel.' Do you find that offensive? I do! People seem so quick to talk about their own experiences, and so the conversation soon turns from your story to them talking about themselves. It may be that they are trying to empathise by telling you about their own story, but these stories rarely make you feel better. Actually, there is no way that they can know how you are feeling because everyone's experience around separation, divorce and loss is unique.

Of course, it's worth noting that when you are feeling strong emotions and dealing with your loss, you are likely to be more sensitive to such comments and more critical of those who are well-meaning. It is hard to blame the people making these comments as they are usually coming from a good place.

At other times, people *do not know what to say*. This can cause them to say nothing at all and at times seemingly avoid you. My client Sophie explained how she felt a real change in the way that people from her children's kindergarten and childcare centre interacted with her post separation.

Sophie felt that once she became a single mother, it was almost as though the 'school mums' no longer knew how to support her or speak with her. She described conversations with these people becoming hurried, very polite but also superficial. Another observation that she shared, which her single friends agreed with, is that other couples would tend to stick together and she no longer received as many invites for social events such as holidays or dinner parties.

GETTING THE RIGHT SUPPORT

I really enjoy the writing of Megan Devine, both in her book and also her website, called Refuge in Grief. Here's an excerpt from a piece she wrote about society's tendency to 'fix' us or avoid us rather than sitting with us during our loss, and allowing us to deal with our loss in our own way and in our own time:

> *'That your world is in pain, that your heart is broken beyond repair, is no reason to turn your back on it. That you witness great pain in someone you care about, that it's hard for you to bear, is no reason to turn your back on them – which is what we do when we ladle on a useless platitude. Trying to make things better, we just make things worse.*
>
> *'... Pain is hard. Being alive will break your heart – in small ways, in large ones, in irreparable ones. And that's okay. That you hurt when life hurts doesn't make you wrong. You don't need to be talked out of your pain. You don't need to be "cheered up." You just need to be heard. It's that simple.'*

You are allowed to experience sorrow. You should be able to feel sadness and anger and depression and uncertainty. Rather than trying to 'fix' you, the best support may be someone just being with you, sitting with you and listening to you.

Another warning on receiving support from family and friends is that you should *not* rely on them for legal advice. While it's common for people to have their own separation and family law stories (which you may never hear the end of), you shouldn't rely on these people for legal advice.

I am disappointed when I hear clients have formed unrealistic expectations about their matter because their friend had a 'similar' matter. Likewise, it is disheartening to hear that a client took so long to receive legal advice because they figured they had 'no chance', since their mate at the pub told them about his nightmare experience of the family law system.

My client Jillian said that one of the first things that she did after separating was ask her friends about their experiences. It was not long before she realised that each matter is different. She said:

> 'Friends and family gave me well-meaning but often conflicting advice... my family and friends were keen to see the best outcome for me, so they related many stories about people they know who had separated. In hindsight, some of it was useful and accurate, while other advice was incorrect. The conflicting advice from family and friends left me feeling quite lost until I gained legitimate input from my lawyer.'

The other point Jillian made was in relation to the Family Law Court process, as her matter unfortunately required litigation. She told me that her well-meaning friends would tell her, at length, what to say at court – but the reality was that the hearings did not require her to talk at all. There was a real mismatch of information given, which is often fed through the public's lack of knowledge of the family law system.

Don't get me wrong – friends and family hold a very important place in your journey. They are there to listen to you and provide emotional support. They may attend meetings with you and assist by taking notes when it all becomes too overwhelming for you to remember. They can make you dinner when you're too exhausted to cook. They can take care of the kids for the day so you can have some quiet time to work through your legal matter. They can attend court and sit next to you. They hopefully will provide a listening ear.

Another way that your family and friends can help you is to recommend any legal professionals that they have personally used. They will know first-hand what a particular lawyer is like to work with, based on their own experience with them. You may also discover which lawyers to avoid!

You may even make new friends as part of your journey. My client Amanda describes how she was able to meet another single mother with two children who were a similar age to hers. They were both in the same court registry and even had the same judge. They found comfort in their new friendship as a safe space to be able to share their pain and frustration. Amanda said she wished everyone could find this type of supportive friendship as it was very therapeutic for her.

SUMMARY

That brings us to the end of chapter four. In the next chapter, we delve into navigating the family law process and system, no matter what stage you are at (in other words, whether you are trying to resolve your matter amicably directly with your ex-partner or whether you are stuck in a litigious battle). But first, here's a summary of the key points discussed in chapter four:

> You should build a good team around you that includes both professionals and non-professionals.

> Rely on your professionals for professional advice, and your family and friends for peer and emotional support.

> Remember that the breakdown of a relationship is likely to be one of the most difficult times of your life. Do not hesitate to reach out for help and support. (In chapter seven, we speak further about prioritising your mental health during this time.)

> You do not need to be 'fixed', despite what you may think or how people might interact with you in the wake of your separation.

CHAPTER FIVE

NAVIGATING THE FAMILY LAW PROCESS

IN ADDITION TO THE LOSS AND GRIEF YOU MAY BE EXPERIENCING as a result of your separation, you are also likely to be feeling other stresses, such as the uncertainty and unpredictability of our family law system.

Family relationship consultant Olivia Kay discussed with me the array of feelings that someone may be experiencing when they separate. She frequently counsels families who have separated and also writes family reports for the courts. According to Olivia, *'every emotion one can put a name to can be experienced following separation, including anger, sadness, jealousy, self-blame, fear, worry, uncertainty, disappointment and confusion.'*

She also states: *'These common feelings that are felt in the post-separation period often re-emerge or become more acute when ex-partners engage in legal disputes. It is not uncommon for these sorts of disputes to erode any prior progress made by adults in integrating these feelings, especially in the acrimonious setting of court proceedings when feelings of degradation and shame are added to the mix.'*

One of the biggest frustrations for clients going through a separation is the lack of certainty in relation to their matter and the unpredictable nature of the family law system. Regardless of whether I am assisting with a property settlement or a parenting matter, there always seems to be some level of uncertainty.

In this chapter, I'll outline some of the key aspects of family law to help you navigate the process and alleviate at least some of the uncertainty. But first, I want to highlight the importance of picking your battles.

GOING TO WAR: IS IT REALLY WORTH IT?

Separation is a difficult time. It is highly emotional. You may do some silly things and lack focus on what is important. When dealing with your ex-partner, a key element in picking your battles, so to speak, is to be mindful of your mental health. In other words, try to remain calm (as much as possible) and focused on the important issues.

As a new law graduate, I recall with fascination a property settlement case whereby I was instructed by my client to write to his ex-wife about the return of a pet turtle. Despite the fact that pets are not determined to be property (that's another topic!), the turtle had a value of around thirty dollars. The cost of my initial letter and subsequent follow-up letter to the other solicitor exceeded the cost of the turtle. Of course, it is not my role to be judgemental. If you instruct me to pursue the return of something of nominal value, then I will do so. However, you need to assess how important this item really is to you.

In a more recent property settlement negotiation, there was a dispute about a small collection of Penfolds Grange wine. Thankfully, my client had a good sense of humour. She was able to recognise that the cost of disputing the small collection – if she and her ex-partner had to go to court – might exceed the cost of the actual wine. She realised she would be better off buying a couple of new bottles and enjoying a nice drink or two!

When picking your battles, you should also beware of well-meaning friends and family members. They are not privy to everything that you are. They are not experiencing the loss that you have. They have not received all of the legal advice that you may have received. Friends and family members can become particularly aggravated about certain things and may encourage you to pursue certain battles, which may drain your purse or cause you further stress.

It is easy for a well-meaning friend or family member to tell you to 'take him for everything' or 'take her to the cleaners'. But, ultimately, they are not paying your legal fees and they are not stuck in what could be a protracted process. These friends and family members are also unlikely to be family lawyers, so they do not know what is realistic from a legal perspective or what the law says should happen. Often, there is a misalignment between what laypeople think is 'fair' and what the law says.

When you are picking your battles in the family law process, you should absolutely draw on the support of your friends and family. But, ultimately, only you know what is best for you and what is most important to you (and what you're prepared to fight for).

I often have a conversation with clients around avoiding litigation and court proceedings at all costs. It is all too easy to think that you will initiate proceedings to obtain court orders in order to get what you want. However, the uncertainty and stress of court can really take its toll.

Before 'going to war', ensure that you understand what is actually involved in court proceedings. Did you know that most property matters (discussed in more detail in the next subtopic) will take a minimum of eighteen months to achieve final orders? Most parenting matters take longer. Did you know that if you do proceed to court, you will be encouraged to file documents outlining your version of the relationship and, essentially, the faults of your ex-partner? This does little to aid any hope of amicable communication at a later date.

It may be that mediation is a better option for you. It may be that a letter from a lawyer, attempting to negotiate without relying on court proceedings, is also a preferred option. Each matter differs in terms of its complexity and your relationship with your ex-partner. However, the ultimate question is whether or not to go to court. You should take some time to reflect on this and avoid going to war if possible.

PROPERTY MATTERS

When it comes to property settlement, there is uncertainty around how the negotiations or proceedings may pan out. With regard to my law firm, it is not uncommon for our property settlement negotiations to take over twelve months. It can be a very slow process in terms of discovery (the exchange of financial details) and negotiating an actual agreement. For those who are in the early stages of separation, this may come as a surprise.

For those who have been separated for some time but are left having this ongoing 'battle' with their ex-partner, it can be excruciating. There is a constant reminder of the failed relationship and of your ex-partner, which is inescapable. If you are negotiating with a lawyer, then they'll most likely want to see all relevant financial statements (such as bank statements, taxation statements, superannuation statements and other financial particulars), and they may require formal property valuations or appraisals (of the family home and any other properties) to be obtained. If there is superannuation splitting, for example, there can be further delays while the superannuation trustee approves orders. All of these small elements of negotiation can cause delay. The uncertain timeframe can indeed be frustrating.

The exception, in relation to property settlement matters, seems to be those matters which have reached the court system, in that property applications follow a particular process. Lawyers are able to give fairly solid advice in terms of the process that is followed and typical timeframes.

We know, for example, that many matters settle at the point of a Conciliation Conference. The objective of a Conciliation Conference is to help you and your ex-partner reach an agreement on the financial issues arising from the breakdown of your relationship, with a view to reaching resolution and agreement. A registrar of the court will assist the parties and their lawyers in the negotiation, and, if an agreement can be reached, then your matter will quickly be removed from the court list with court proceedings finalised.

If property matters do not settle at that point, then we know that, ultimately, the matter will be listed for final hearing (trial) for judicial determination. The timeframe is relatively predictable. What is not predictable is the outcome if your matter is not resolved during the proceedings by consent. Unfortunately, once a matter is in court, and if no agreement can be reached during that process, then the decision making falls with the judicial officer and you have lost power to control your matter as much as you may have previously.

PARENTING MATTERS

I find parenting matters to be even more unpredictable than property matters. If no agreement can be reached via family dispute resolution (mediation) or negotiation, then the matter is likely to end up in court. Unfortunately, there are so many grey areas around the timetable for a parenting matter and some matters will be in the court list for two years prior to a final hearing. Variables will include:

- How parties behave during the proceedings,

- The outcome of any meeting with a family consultant,

- Recommendations of a single expert,

- Views of any Independent Children's Lawyer,

- Outcomes in terms of both parties' compliance with the orders, and

- How proactive the parties are in ensuring that they progress their matter.

One of the difficulties with parenting matters is that it is very rare that the judicial officer can make a 'finding of fact' on an interim basis. An example of a 'finding of fact' is where the judge is satisfied or convinced that one party is definitely in a violent relationship, a finding that there has been child abuse by one of the parties, or a finding that one parent has alienated the other parent. It is only when the full matter is presented at final hearing (trial) that findings are generally made. That process involves testing the evidence through cross-examination of the parties and their respective witnesses. The result is that the court will generally take a cautious approach on an interim basis. And if there are any concerns in relation to the welfare of a child, then they will make interim orders so as to protect that child.

An example of the unpredictable nature of parenting matters is the experience of my client Dan. Dan faced false allegations of child sexual abuse, made in relation to his son. The result of this was waiting for the Department of Child Protection to complete an investigation – and make a finding that there was, in fact, no abuse or risk – prior to the Family Law Court being satisfied that the child was not at risk. For Dan, this essentially meant that any time with his son was put on hold pending that process. As you can imagine, this sort of issue can be incredibly frustrating and stressful.

FOLLOWING AN AGREEMENT OR COURT ORDER

You may have been fortunate enough to reach an agreement with your ex-partner without a mediation service or the use of lawyers. If you've reached a verbal or written agreement, your ongoing task is *complying* with that agreement.

If you and your ex-partner have agreed on things such as who will leave the family home, handover times of the children, telephone contact numbers, communication expectations, and the time the kids spend with each of you, then it is usually worth sticking to that agreement. If you want to vary an agreement, then you should be transparent about that with your ex-partner. If you do not intend to do what you said you would do, then your ex-partner should be informed (whether that is through you or via a lawyer – whichever is more appropriate).

If you do not respect any agreement reached and do not adequately communicate the reason for non-compliance with your ex-partner, then it is more than likely going to cause issues with your ongoing relationship. An amicable separation can turn difficult and nasty quite quickly in those circumstances.

Formal agreements can be reached a number of ways and recorded via a Parenting Plan, Heads of Agreement, Binding Financial Agreement, Consent Minutes of Order or court order (which may not necessarily be an 'agreement' but rather a judicial decision). Regardless of the type of agreement, it is rarely in your interest not to comply.

A Parenting Plan is an informal agreement that is written

and signed by you and your ex-partner. They are frequently used at community mediation services. If you do not comply with a Parenting Plan, then your ex-partner may initiate court proceedings to enforce the Parenting Plan or, alternatively, seek orders that are less favourable than the agreement set out in the Parenting Plan.

An example of this is where I see parents having reached their own informal agreement without legal advice. They may, for example, have agreed on a 'shared care' or fifty/fifty type arrangement. It may be that, realistically, the court does not consider that type of arrangement to be suitable for the children, and, as a result, the judicial officer makes an order that provides for the children to live with one parent the majority of the time.

If you do not comply with parenting orders (orders made by the court), then your matter may end up back in court via a Contravention Application or Application in a Case. These applications are made by one party, asserting that the other party has breached orders. Remedies include:

- Enforcement of time (to ensure that parties are spending time with children as the court has ordered)

- Makeup time (to provide extra time for parents who have missed out on court-ordered time)

- Variation of the orders

- Financial penalty

Ongoing litigation is not in anyone's interest. The judicial officers do not respond well to parties breaching orders in relation to parenting matters, and they have the jurisdiction to vary final orders if it is in the best interest of the children to do so.

If you have breached or contravened a court order, be aware that contravention proceedings are quasi criminal. The applicant needs to prove that the orders were breached and that there was no 'reasonable excuse' for doing so. I have seen severe penalties, including imprisonment (notably, this is rare!). However, it is something that you need to be aware of.

At times, it is necessary to breach a court order. Examples of where it may be considered necessary or a reasonable excuse to breach parenting orders would be where there are new allegations of child assault, fresh concerns around drug use, new involvement from the Department of Child Protection, or if one party has re-partnered and is now in a violent domestic relationship. However, you should always obtain legal advice beforehand with a view to avoiding having to return to court.

If you do not comply with the terms of a property-related Binding Financial Agreement or consent orders for property settlement, then you may find yourself served with enforcement proceedings and a cost order against you. If there is a genuine reason for non-compliance in a parenting or property matter, then it is usually best to communicate this with your lawyer and also your ex-partner. If you have a lawyer, they will probably put something in writing for you, thus creating a 'paper trail' to show that there is a genuine reason and also that you have made all attempts to properly communicate this with your ex-partner.

FLAWS IN THE SYSTEM

The family law system is problematic and due for a proper overhaul. The original *Family Law Act* came into effect in 1975 and is outdated. In 1996, we saw amendments that focused on the need to consider more seriously the protection of children from family violence. There were further reforms in 2006, including 'shared parenting objectives'. Those reforms were based on research showing that children benefit from a meaningful relationship with both parents.

While nobody can disagree with that reasoning (presuming the child is not at risk and there are no welfare concerns), the *Shared Parental Responsibility Act* has caused a lot of controversy and debate. It has also created unrealistic expectations of parents being able to achieve equal custody, including an expectation that the court would or should make orders for equal shared time or what some people refer to as 'fifty/fifty'.

I still hear clients talk about the 'right' to equal time and their unrealistic views around what a court may order. These views are largely drawn from what is heard from friends or family, or read on a forum. The reality is that the family law system remains grossly unsatisfactory. We need reforms which better support parties to negotiate and resolve their matters outside of the court setting. We need more judicial officers to deal with matters in the court system – the delays can be appalling!

ARE LAWYERS PARTLY TO BLAME?

The other frustration that I have with our current 'system', which you may also have experienced, is that the chances of resolving the matter by consent, or reducing the time the parties are in negotiation or litigation, may be dependent on the particular lawyers instructed. Let's face it – lawyers do not necessarily have a great reputation among the general public!

While many lawyers do try to resolve matters with their client's best interest at the forefront, there are some firms that are money-grubbing. As an example of this, some matters will end up in court when it really is not necessary. Other court matters will be more protracted than necessary and there will be more documents filed than required. At other times, there will be more time spent negotiating outcomes for parties than may be necessary. Again – more uncertainties!

You may also have experienced frustration from dealing with law firms that have bombarded you with correspondence and last-minute court documents. My frustrations with the cost and approach of some lawyers, and tips for saving money in that respect, led me to pen another book on this exact topic.

STORIES FROM THE FRONTLINE

As someone who has recently separated, you not only have to navigate this uncertainty and unsatisfactory family law system but also deal with the emotions of the actual separation. It's no wonder you are confused and stressed! This is completely understandable and normal. In fact, many of my clients have felt this way.

My client Sophie said that while she had confidence in me as her lawyer, in terms of my ability and empathy, she *never* felt a sense of certainty. Her matter was in the Family Law Court system for two years. During that entire time, she felt an underlying sense of uncertainty and felt as though her fate was *'entirely in the court's hands'.*

Another client, Jillian, said, *'In the weeks preceding the court case, I hardly slept, and I couldn't think of anything else. It was difficult to concentrate. I felt physically ill, with tightness in the chest, nausea and headaches. I would have never thought that stress and emotional pain could cause such illness.'*

Jillian went on to say that despite feeling incredibly supported by her legal team, and also considering herself a professional and intelligent person, the system was *'anything but predictable'* and that she felt *'a complete lack of control'.*

When I interviewed my client Jane for this book, she was just about to embark on her journey into the Family Law Courts. Her ex-husband initiated proceedings and was seeking, in my view, very unreasonable parenting orders. Jane was kind and brave enough to have a long conversation with me at this point. When I asked her how she was feeling, she said:

> *'I'm feeling very scared and anxious and angry at having to hear him talk about stuff that is not true, and I am worried about how I will react to hearing crap and*

> sitting across from him with that smug look on his face, like, "Well, I told you." I'm scared about court. I'm scared they will say I am crazy – "So we'll give the kids to dad" – and treat me like a criminal even though I haven't done anything. He even told the mediator that I am an abusive parent, which is wrong and just shameful.'

Jane felt particularly angry that she had ended up in court when there was no drug use, no welfare concerns and no family violence allegations. She wrongfully thought that only people from a low socioeconomic background ended up in court; this was her experience from having been a school teacher.

As a family lawyer, my job is to navigate the 'system' as best as possible on behalf of my clients. Having practised in this jurisdiction for close to twenty years, I am able to position clients quite well in terms of giving them guidance as to what to expect in relation to their particular matter (despite the uncertainties).

During a first meeting, it is very common for clients to start the conversation with 'You will not believe my story' or 'You probably haven't heard anything as bad as my separation'. To be honest, it is quite rare that I am surprised these days, given the amount of family law matters I have been exposed to. Having said that, every single matter is unique, and everyone's difficulty, stress and loss needs to be treated individually and sensitively.

SUMMARY

That brings us to the end of chapter five. In the next chapter, I discuss further ways that you can remain in control of your separation, and also give you specific examples to help you take control if you are trying to navigate the family law system. But first, here's a summary of the key points discussed in chapter five:

> Navigating the family law system can create a lot of uncertainty, given its unpredictable nature.

> Consider whether you are prepared to make concessions with your ex-partner when negotiating your property or parenting matter. What is truly important to you? Pick your battles!

> Always negotiate and mediate as an alternative to going to court. This tends to cause less financial stress and you are also likely to remain more in control of the outcome.

> There are many flaws in our family law system. Unfortunately, we need to work within those parameters as we are unable to change the law or change the system.

CHAPTER SIX

TAKING BACK CONTROL

The keyword in the title of this chapter is <u>control</u>. When going through a separation and experiencing the loss of your family, you can feel as though your life is completely out of control. There may be times when you feel *in* control, but other times when you feel as though you have completely lost your way. And, to be perfectly honest, there are definitely things that you simply can't control during this time in your life.

Something that I frequently tell my clients is that they do not have control over how their ex-partner deals with the separation. No matter how you style your approach or the tactics you use, the way in which your ex-partner responds or engages is simply out of your control. You can't control how they behave and how they communicate with you.

My client Sophie described to me the appalling conduct of her husband at the time of their separation. The family home was to be sold by the bank due to thousands of dollars in unpaid debt, which Sophie's husband had accumulated during the marriage without her knowledge or consent. The discovery of the debt, and being informed of the forcible property sale, was devastating for her.

On top of that, her husband threatened her by indicating that she would be hearing from the Department of Welfare, which would be removing the children from her care. He cited the fact that she no longer had a home and could not financially support the children. The appalling behaviour of Sophie's husband was outside of her control.

However, I think it is helpful to consider the things that you *can* control when going through your loss and perhaps the stress of the family law system. The best advice I can give you, from a family law perspective, is to control what you can control.

For example, you can control, to a certain extent, how you *react* to the process. A wise social worker (my late dad) would always tell me that nobody has the power to control how you *feel* and nobody else is responsible for how you react to things. How you respond, react and what you feel is your choice. I found the advice of my father quite frustrating when I was growing up, but now that I am older and presumably wiser, I think the old man was on to something!

Let's delve into some practical things that you can do to feel more in control of your separation and loss.

TAKE SOME TIME

People going through a separation, and the subsequent feelings of loss and grief, are often told to take their time, to do things their way and at a pace they can manage. Pick up any piece of literature on grieving the loss of a loved one, and you'll be told that you cannot rush the stages of loss and grief, and that there may be days when you're not able to function.

Unfortunately, in the context of family law, you are not given the opportunity to take things at your own pace. If dealing with a property settlement, then there are time limitations that need to be considered. If you have mediation scheduled, then you need to be well prepared. If your lawyer is writing a letter to your ex-partner, then they will likely want relevant documents in a timely matter, or for you to settle certain correspondence.

If your matter ends up in the Family Law Courts, then the judicial officer will set the timeline for you. You will have to meet deadlines for filing documents and attending court hearings. You may have appointments with your lawyer, mental health professionals or a family report writer. Not surprisingly, this can all start to feel very stressful.

I am aware that when I represent clients either through a negotiation or mediation process, or via court proceedings, the demand I place on them can be perceived as unreasonable. Legal practitioners need to ensure they are well prepared for negotiation or mediation, or that they are complying with court orders.

However, it may seem that your lawyer is overly demanding in terms of the information that they are requesting from you or the short turnaround to complete certain tasks. I have had clients who say they feel the need to take extended leave from their employment because dealing with the demands of the family law system is like a full-time job.

I am aware that it is not just the day of mediation or the day that you meet with your lawyer that you may need off work. The reality is that you likely feel so engrossed in your separation that you are mentally distracted from your job, either in the lead-up to a specific event or after such an event (or both). For example, how productive are you likely to be the day before a mediation session or the day before a court hearing?

If you are an employee, you are unlikely to have an unlimited amount of leave available, so you need to think carefully about the amount of time you take off. Also, keep in mind that each employer is likely to respond differently in terms of how much support and understanding they provide. Taking leave without pay might be an option worth considering, providing it doesn't cause too much financial stress. Have you been subjected to family violence? The Fair Work Ombudsman has released an Employer Guide to Family and Domestic Violence to support employees. The guide highlights the fact that an employee living with family and domestic violence is often experiencing heightened financial stress and is at greater risk of homelessness, vulnerability and also a sense of shame. Your employer has an obligation in terms of minimum entitlements for unpaid family and domestic violence leave.

You are also entitled to request flexible working arrangements and, in some circumstances, take paid or unpaid personal or carer's leave. The Fair Work Act enables employees dealing with family violence to take five days of unpaid leave for each twelve-month period. If you are requesting a flexible working arrangement, then you need to have been employed for twelve continuous months *prior to* requesting the leave.

If you are seeking leave under this provision, or if you want to disclose to your employer the reason for taking other leave, then you'll have to disclose some basic details to your employer. Your employer is entitled to request evidence in support of your request, which may include court or police documents.

If you are self-employed or a small business owner, then you may have more flexibility with your working hours and may find it easier to work around your family law commitments. You may also be able to work around your good days and your not-so-good days. I know I've had days where I have felt such sorrow that I have not been able to function well, so I've worked at other hours to make up the time.

BE ORGANISED

One of the most helpful things that you can do is to remain as organised as possible. Please do not be one of those clients who comes into your lawyer's office with a shopping bag full of documents! Worse still, if you are navigating separation or the legal system yourself, then you will not know which documents you are looking for or how to find them quickly and easily. Organisation can give you a greater sense of control of your situation.

I suggest you start keeping a notebook purely for your separation. You can start writing relevant notes, which you can refer to later if need be. Take notes when you receive legal advice or when you speak to your financial adviser. Take notes when you speak to any service provider. The types of notes would include, usually in chronological order, the date of the conversation, contact phone numbers, the name of the person that you spoke to, and any main points or advice received. If you are speaking to different counsellors, service providers, lawyers and so on, then keep all of your notes together. You will otherwise likely get confused or forget information. This is a good idea even if your separation has been amicable.

If there is likely to be a property settlement, then start putting together a chronology of events, including the date of purchase of real estate, property values and so on. You should also keep all bank statements, superannuation statements and other financial documents in order by holding them in a hardcopy folder or electronic folders. These documents are what we call discovery material. If you are negotiating a matrimonial or de facto property settlement, then they will likely need to be exchanged at some point, even if your separation has been relatively amicable.

My preference is electronic folders that are labelled (such as 'bank statements', 'accounting', 'superannuation', and so on). However, even having a hardcopy folder with documents in the same section can be helpful. This not only helps you to feel as though you are in greater control, but also can be of immense assistance to your solicitor. It may also reduce the time spent by your legal team and, in turn, reduce any legal fees.

WHERE THERE'S A WILL, THERE'S A WAY

Once you and your partner decide to separate, you should update your will and any documents relating to your Estate. If you don't have a will, you should seriously consider having one drafted.

Keep in mind that separation itself does not rescind your will. If you were married, then divorce may revoke your will. However, there is still uncertainty surrounding your Estate. You want to avoid your Estate being distributed under the laws of intestacy as opposed to your express wishes. (Intestacy means that the law of your particular state sets out who should be the executor to administer your Estate (including your ex-partner!) and who the beneficiaries would be.) In other words, you need to update your will to ensure that you have nominated the right beneficiaries. I suspect your ex-partner is no longer one of them.

You also want to ensure that the executor of your Estate is someone nominated by you. Again, I suspect you do not want your ex-partner controlling your Estate upon your death. You should also turn your mind to nominating guardians of any children. A family lawyer (as discussed in chapter four) can help you draft and/or update your will accordingly.

You should also ensure that you have a Power of Attorney and Advance Care Directives in place. These documents stipulate whom you appoint to take care of your legal and medical decisions in the event that you are unable to do so. Presumably, you want to ensure that you exclude your ex-partner from being appointed under law in the event that you do not have these documents in order!

Having all three of these documents in place and updated accordingly will provide some peace of mind and further control of your situation.

Even if there is no dispute in relation to your property division or other financial matters, you can still control how organised you are moving forward with all things finance-related. Previously, you and your ex-partner may have jointly dealt with finances. Or perhaps your ex-partner largely dealt with all of the finances. Either way, the more organised you can be moving forward, the better. It will mean one less thing to worry about and one more thing that you can feel as though you have control over.

If there is a dispute in relation to children and parenting matters, then start keeping notes in a notebook immediately – even if things are amicable at this point. This is generally my advice to clients when they first approach me for legal advice and their separation is relatively fresh. Hopefully, your matter is not in court or will not reach that point. However, it may be that there is litigation and/or a dispute in the future.

The notebook may be as simple as jotting down the times that you have had the children in your care, or the time that your ex-partner has spent with the children. You may record the dates and times of telephone calls if there is no regular pattern of telephone calls. If the children are struggling with handovers, then you may keep a written record of this. If you have received some legal advice or made contact with a mediation service, then write that down in your notebook in chronological order (or in an organised manner that makes sense to you). Keep all of the names of the people that you speak to, and their contact details, so as to ensure that you can easily access the information at a later date if need be.

It is difficult to remember these specific details further down the track, particularly as you try to deal with the emotional toll of the separation. Your children are presumably the most precious thing in your life. So when it comes to disputes around children, keeping a notebook of all relevant details will ensure you don't forget anything important. It can also help to provide perspective and clarification for any mediation process that may take place.

My client Jillian was advised by her brother to start writing down everything that she could remember, and also to search for and keep a record of relevant documents and receipts. In other words, to be as organised as possible! One outcome of this approach was that it gave Jillian some direction. She said to me, *'I felt like I was "doing something" in that stressful time.'* The act of collating and organising will help you feel as though you are doing everything that you can to stay in control.

ARM YOURSELF WITH KNOWLEDGE

Arming yourself with knowledge is twofold. Firstly, in relation to the family law system and, secondly, in relation to loss and grief.

I am pleased that you are reading this book and sincerely hope that it is offering some insight in relation to the loss that you are experiencing. I suspect that unless you have previously experienced the loss of a relationship or family unit, you may not have much knowledge of this form of grief. Nobody teaches you how to deal with the breakdown of a relationship, nor is it something that you usually turn your mind to until you are experiencing it yourself. The fact that you are taking time out for yourself to read this book and arm yourself with further knowledge should be empowering in itself.

One of the single most important things you can do to remain in control during the family law process is to obtain legal advice prior to separation. It is quite rare that we see clients at this point, but we certainly applaud those who do see us! It does not necessarily follow that the client proceeds with the separation.

However, I suspect the majority of people reading this book have already separated from their partners, so this advice has come too late. But if you *are* contemplating separation, be sure to obtain legal advice prior to leaving the relationship (if you are able to do so). Just because you obtain legal advice doesn't mean that you will engage a lawyer, but it does ensure that you have some basic information about what your rights are and what the process would involve.

Even if your separation is amicable and you have reached an agreement, you should still arm yourself with knowledge so as to formalise the agreement and protect your interests moving forward.

If you've already separated, I recommend obtaining independent legal advice as soon as possible. If you have not instructed a solicitor, then you may want to approach a free legal service in the first instance, such as your legal aid commission or a community legal service.

Legal aid has strict criteria to qualify for ongoing legal funding and you have to fall within their guidelines. For example, they generally do not provide funding for property settlements, interstate relocation of children, or for permission to travel overseas with your children (if that is in dispute). Legal aid will be means and merit tested so you will need to establish that you are in financial hardship and also that you have merit in your application. If you do not qualify for ongoing advice, then I recommend meeting with at least two private solicitors to obtain advice specific to your matter. You also want to assess whether they are a good fit for you in terms of any future work that may be required.

My client Jillian reported that, prior to separation, she had no idea about the family law system. In retrospect, she wished that she had armed herself with more information at that time and sought professional help earlier. Jillian also reported that the advice she received from the first lawyer she saw was incorrect, and that she regrets not seeking input from more than one solicitor initially before heading down a path where she was misinformed.

I have already discussed the dangers of relying on well-meaning friends and family members for legal advice. If they have been through separation and loss, then they can provide *emotional* support (but that's all). Similarly, when arming yourself with knowledge, please avoid relying on internet searches or 'Lawyer Google' too much. As I explained in chapter four, I am involved in a few online forums where men and women provide support to each other through their separation and loss. While many of these online forums are well-intended and do indeed offer much-needed support, I remain very concerned about some of the information I see in these forums, as it is simply incorrect.

If you have a lawyer, then ask them to provide you with any references or articles that might be relevant to your specific matter. My law firm has a number of videos on various topics that we provide to clients, depending on what stage they are at in their separation. We also run regular webinars to properly educate the public.

If you do not have a lawyer, then you may want to read legal blogs or information from legal websites. Again, my law firm produces many helpful videos on social media and also YouTube. These videos are presented in a way that is informative and accessible to the layperson. I have purposely created the content in this way, as I am mindful that lawyers tend to speak in 'legalese', and, as a result, navigating and understanding the law as a layperson can be ridiculously confusing.

The other excellent way to arm yourself with knowledge and support is to link in with services such as Relationships Australia or the Family Relationship Centres. Both are government funded and often the first port of call for separation advice, counselling referrals, parenting course referrals, anger management course referrals and mediation services.

There are also many parenting courses, which can be particularly useful if you want to improve your parenting skills and also improve your co-parenting skills. The Circle of Security International Parenting Course is excellent and highly recommended to all parents. It can help to address your children's attachment issues and build emotional resilience, which is particularly important post separation. The course also helps you to understand your children's needs and emotions, and to ensure they feel secure. Regardless of whether or not you have separated from your partner, or are considering separating, this course can give you a better understanding of your children's needs and relationships.

My experience is that many clients are hesitant to complete a parenting course. Afterwards, however, they almost always say they found the course useful. My advice is that you should consider these types of parenting courses even if your matter is not in court or is not court ordered. Many of them are free and can be completed online.

If your matter is likely to be litigated, then you are putting your best foot forward by completing these courses prior to your matter being court ordered. You can even suggest that your ex-partner complete the courses as well, if you find them beneficial. They may even help you to communicate more effectively with your ex-partner.

WEAR YOUR BUSINESS HAT

Are you able to think of your separation as a business transaction? I know it's easier said than done. But if you can try to remove at least some of the emotion from it, this will help you through the process.

I tell clients to try and put on their 'business hats' when dealing with all things in relation to their separation. As much as possible, remain civil and courteous with both your ex-partner and also your lawyer, if you have one. Maintaining civil communication can contribute to the successful resolution of any property or parenting matter. If you can both remain civil, then it is also likely to reduce any feelings of stress.

In a pre-mediation session, a social worker advised my client,

Amanda, to treat her ex-partner in a businesslike fashion. Be businesslike, be formal, be direct and be polite. In my view, this is not only important in relation to face-to-face communication, but all forms of written communication as well. Keep in mind that, from time to time (if not frequently), you will be met with terse and rude communication. You need to do your best to keep any response polite and businesslike.

My friend Rylie spoke about how he and his ex-partner have communicated post separation. They run businesses together, so their separation was even more complex. He said that he and his ex-partner made a conscious decision to put their business hats on. In doing so, they've been able to remove the emotion from their conversations, and treat their business and investment property portfolio (which includes at least twelve properties) as a business transaction.

If you decide to communicate with your ex-partner, then please <u>do not</u> show them copies of any correspondence or written advice that your lawyer has sent to you, and do not show them any draft documents which are not intended for them until finalised. It is a positive sign that you would like to keep the lines of communication open with your ex-partner. However, you also need to protect your position (whether it be financial or in relation to parenting matters).

Also be mindful that anything you write to your partner via email, text message or social media that doesn't go through your lawyer is not done so on a 'without prejudice' basis, meaning that it may be annexed to a court affidavit if your matter ends up in court. Lawyers often draft correspondence and offers on a 'without prejudice basis', meaning that the other party is precluded from revealing the contents of the correspondence to the court. This allows us to exchange letters of negotiation and proposals for settlement without the risk of it being shown to the court at a later date if we do not reach an agreement. This protects your position and is also designed to encourage negotiation. It encourages proposals to be exchanged that are perhaps more generous and more pragmatic than a formal position would be in the court process.

In relation to some of the smaller decisions or issues that concern your ex-partner, see if you can communicate with them directly rather than involving a lawyer. For example, if you have children, do you really need your lawyer to write to the other party about the children's extracurricular activities or particular issues in relation to their schooling? These are the sorts of things that you may include in a communication book, which you exchange with your ex-partner at handover. Sometimes, you absolutely will need support from your lawyer to address some of these smaller issues. However, remember what we discussed in chapter five about the importance of picking your battles.

There's no denying that communicating with your ex-partner can be difficult – particularly if they are not also trying their best to be civil. I asked Paul Ellis, counsellor and owner of Renewal Counselling, for his tips on communicating with a partner or ex-partner. He said, wherever possible, to try to avoid blaming the other person, and try to manage your own thoughts and emotions.

To do this, be mindful of the language you use when

communicating with your ex-partner. Paul suggests using phrases such as, 'I feel X because of Y' and 'I would prefer X'. This can be a more effective way of expressing your feelings, rather than simply pointing the blame at your ex-partner. You should also be mindful of your body language, avoiding negative gestures such as eye rolling.

Ultimately, you have to find a way to communicate that works best for you (and your ex-partner).

Olivia Kay says that one really important way to effectively communicate with your ex-partner, if you have children together, is to both identify and share what your values are in terms of being a separated parent. She gave examples such as ensuring the children remain at their current school, or that both parents continue to attend sporting events, or that handovers are kept civil and polite. The values that are important to you and your ex-partner may be completely different, so it is important to be able to express and share what is important to you both. Olivia says:

> *'Keeping these values in mind, and making sure the other parent knows and agrees to accept these values, can act as a self-reminder when feelings of loss can come to the fore. Identifying and sharing them in the first instance also means that reminding the other parent when communication is not staying true to these values does not become a slanging match or an exercise in blaming the other.'*

One of my clients, Jillian, had no direct communication with her ex-husband at all; all communication was via lawyers. This was her choice because she found it too upsetting to communicate directly with her ex-husband – particularly as the communication had been threatening and abusive in the past.

My client Liarne finds that texting works best with her ex-husband, particularly with regard to issues relating to their children. Initially, Liarne tried to talk to her ex-husband face to face, but he would either be non-responsive or they would always get into an argument. Sometimes, the conversation would take a turn away from the children or what she was trying to communicate. By texting, Liarne can ensure that her messages are always courteous and remain on point.

My client Dan – who is working on re-building trust with his ex-partner after they ended up in court – said the key is to avoid writing text messages or emails that are emotionally charged, particularly in the early stages of separation when both people are likely to be grieving.

My client John said that he and his ex-partner have been able to communicate quite well post separation, simply because their children are always with them when they see each other. His advice is simple: *'Always think about your children and how your actions will affect them.'*

I asked Pete Nicholls for any tips he had on communication post separation. Here are his 'golden nuggets':

- Never respond to anything that you find upsetting or annoying without having a) sat on it for twenty-four hours and b) discussed it with someone else whom you can trust. As a general rule of thumb, when replying to any correspondence with your ex-partner, ask yourself: What would my kids think of this message if they viewed it as adults?

- Keep it BIFF (brief, informative, friendly and firm)!

- Keep it in writing until you're *both* able to manage your emotions in a real-time exchange.

- Avoid using the word 'you' in either written or spoken exchanges. It's nearly always accusatory in this context, and removing it forces you to think objectively about what it is that you're trying to say.

MEDIATE AND NEGOTIATE (DON'T LITIGATE!)

To a certain extent, whether you mediate or litigate is not something that you will have complete control of. If your ex-partner is unwilling to communicate, or your communication is very toxic, then it may be that mediation or family dispute resolution is not appropriate for you. In Australia, the *Family Law Act* stipulates that you must attempt to mediate prior to initiating court proceedings.

There are exceptions, such as when your matter is urgent or where there has been family violence. The court would consider a matter urgent, and would therefore 'bypass' the need for mediation, if, for example, one party moved interstate with a child (without the permission of the other party), or the Department of Child Protection became involved with the family due to care and welfare concerns for children. Keep in mind that your sense and definition of 'urgency' will differ from the court's definition!

It is always my preference to keep clients out of court so as to minimise their legal fees and also stress. That said, there occasionally comes a time when negotiations, mediations or informal conferences are not progressing and a judicial decision is required. It can help to instruct a solicitor who is experienced in negotiating rather than having a reputation of litigating, as a reasonable agreement is more likely to be reached through negotiations and a collaborative approach.

If you are not instructing a solicitor, or are only receiving some limited advice from a private lawyer or community legal aid lawyer, then one of the things that may be useful for you is to initiate the family dispute resolution process yourself. There are low-cost community mediation services, such as Relationships Australia, and also a number of private services, which are pricier but can generally help you sooner.

If you take the initiative to commence this process, then it is more likely to keep things amicable with your ex-partner, as it shows that you are making a genuine attempt to resolve your property and/or parenting matter without being litigious. It may be that your ex-partner refuses to participate or that the actual mediation is fruitless. However, it is still worth trying.

I often negotiate rather than litigate for clients who have been a victim of family violence or an accused perpetrator of family violence. This includes matters where there is an Intervention Order or an Apprehended Violence Order (AVO) in place. I will also attend lawyer-assisted mediation with them in these circumstances – usually run as a 'shuttle conference' (meaning that you and your lawyer are in one room, and your ex-partner is in another room). The chairperson will move back and forward between the two of you, exchanging ideas and proposals.

When a client is legally represented, they are less likely to be affected by coercive, controlling behaviour, and this can be a good way forward rather than proceeding to court. A lawyer can ensure that any agreement reached provides further protection for children and an alleged victim of violence. We can include various injunctions in any agreement, such as preventing one party from going to the family home or the children's school, preventing denigration of each other, preventing discussing certain things in the presence of the children, and so on.

It is my view that the way the Family Law Courts are structured is severely flawed in how they protect victims of violence, and that the whole process is often way too drawn out and, therefore, re-traumatises a victim. The Family Law Courts are designed to require the use of affidavit material as evidence in chief, meaning that all evidence and information before the court early on in the proceedings is through an affidavit, which outlines details of the relationship and concerns around parenting or property matters. Victims of family violence are required to detail incidents of family violence, which in itself can be a traumatic experience.

It is also quite rare, particularly at interim hearing stage, for the court to be closed and private. The Family Law Courts are open to the public, meaning that evidence via affidavit material is frequently spoken of in court through submissions and also judicial officer comment. While some courts have 'safe rooms', where family violence victims can sit prior to their matter being called on, it is my experience that victims are still required to sit in the courtroom during the actual hearing.

In 2019, the Commonwealth introduced new legislation whereby a perpetrator of family violence is no longer able to directly cross-examine the alleged victim if they are self-represented. However, this is only applicable to the cross-examination component at trial (the 'pointy end' of the proceedings). No allowance is made in the period prior to reaching trial (typically eighteen months to two years), during which time a victim is constantly re-traumatised throughout the court process.

Also, my observation is that even if a perpetrator of family violence is not personally cross-examining an alleged victim, having a barrister cross-examine them is still an extremely traumatic experience. If you are required to go to court and you are a victim of family violence, one thing that you can control is ensuring your legal team is experienced in the area of family violence, and sensitive to your experience and your needs. A family violence worker may be able to recommend a lawyer who will be sensitive to your situation and really provide you with the necessary guidance throughout the court process.

CAP YOUR LEGAL COSTS

One way to create certainty and retain some control around

your separation and, if applicable, family law matter is in relation to your legal fees. Fixed fees are certainly one approach that my firm offers, with the benefit being that it offers complete transparency.

The type of work completed by lawyers is very complex, so it's not uncommon for more time to be spent on your matter than initially thought. Lawyers can spend hours reading through discovery documents to find key information, which may, in fact, save you thousands of dollars in the long run. The beauty of fixed fees is that you're aware of the cost from the outset, so there's no nasty bill shock.

As the client, you receive a scope of work that will be completed for a fixed fee. This means you're not 'watching the clock' for every six-minute interval to pass (most law firms traditionally charge for all of the work that they do in six-minute intervals or part thereof, which can create a terrible lawyer/client relationship)! You're not dreading every interim invoice, with no idea how much work has been done. Fixed fees are relevant at all stages of negotiation, including mediation and informal conferences, with a view to keeping your matter out of court. If your matter does end up requiring court proceedings, then fixed fees are charged for each stage of the proceedings or for a certain timeframe so that you still have certainty in those circumstances.

Are you asset rich but cash poor? Do you feel as though you may be entitled to a sizeable portion of your property settlement but have no way of paying the potential legal fees? Perhaps you were not the main 'breadwinner' in the relationship and, now that you have separated, you are surviving on either a Centrelink benefit or a single low income. You should not let this stop you from reaching out for assistance.

Some law firms will offer clients a deferred fee cost agreement, meaning that you do not need to pay for your legal fees upfront. Instead, your legal fees will be taken from your anticipated cash payout in the settlement. It may be that the family home is likely to be sold and you are to receive funds from the proceeds of sale. You may also qualify for a grant of legal aid. If you're unsure, you should speak to a lawyer or your state's legal aid service.

BATCH TASKS AS NECESSARY

Many of my clients are so grief-stricken and overwhelmed by their loss that they struggle to communicate, meet deadlines and generally deal with the logistics of their separation. I've had clients who are notorious for not answering telephone calls or checking messages – no doubt because they find the whole experience too upsetting. If you are able to 'batch' tasks, setting them aside for when you feel mentally strong enough to complete them, then this can be a good coping mechanism.

Another way to describe batching is to *compartmentalise*. This involves separating things into smaller categories to feel more in control and to make things more manageable. Compartmentalising can be particularly useful when you are in the deep stages of grief, including depression, and your energy is depleted.

Some days, you may wake up knowing that there is no way that you will have a productive day, and other days, you may wake up fired up and ready to go. By batching or compartmentalising, you'll allow yourself to get on with things on your good days when you know you will be in the right mindset. This is an important part of self-care (which we'll discuss in more detail in chapter eight).

Receiving emails and letters can act as a 'trigger' and a reminder of your loss. There is no doubt that you will receive constant reminders of your ex-partner and your loss. Perhaps there are joint assets or joint bills. Perhaps mail has not been redirected. Perhaps the children's school is emailing you both concurrently. Your accountant may be in contact. The bank. The list goes on.

One client recently said to me, *'No offence, but I hated receiving your emails!'* I know that it is quite rare for a client to enjoying speaking with a lawyer. I imagine it's a similar story when speaking to a financial adviser or mediator. In light of this, I strongly recommend setting up a separate email address, used solely for correspondence in relation to your separation. This may be the same email address that you use to communicate with your ex-partner. The reality is that if you use your personal or work email address to deal with issues around your separation, then you will struggle to 'shut off' or compartmentalise.

I have personally used batching as a coping mechanism for grief. I have, for example, allowed all of my deceased parents' mail to build up before opening it all at once on a day that I am feeling up to it. Processing the estates of both parents at the same time has also required numerous difficult and also frustrating telephone calls. I have been known to allow calls to go to voicemail and then return a number of calls all at once when I am having a 'good day'.

BE GRATEFUL (YES, REALLY!)

Why me?

Have you asked yourself this question? If you have, I'm not surprised.

Many people who have experienced a loss such as separation ask, 'Why me?' It is not uncommon for there to be a victim mentality and, at times, a self-pity party. You've likely had a self-pity party at some stage! It is to be expected. The concern is when the pity party continues and you allow the pain to *define* you. You allow yourself to become a victim. Perhaps you identify yourself as a 'single mother' or 'alienated father', for example.

There is a lot to be said around the chemistry of gratitude. Rather than asking, 'Why me?' have you considered a different perspective? Other questions you could ask yourself, or statements you could say to yourself, include:

- Why not me?

- I'm lucky for the time I had.

- I am grateful to have X, Y or Z.

- I am lucky to have the kids.

- Why do I allow the pain to define me?

Practising gratitude can really help you reduce your stress levels. If your cortisone levels are high, then you are unlikely to be making good decisions! It can also help you deal with the pain you're feeling. How you 'own' your pain and approach a good or bad day says a lot about your self-identity. Owning your pain does not mean that you do not feel pain, or that you try to ignore it or downplay it. It means not allowing the pain to *define* you, or rushing through the pain. In other words, you acknowledge the pain for what it is and allow yourself to feel it when you have to.

I have recently started a gratitude journal, which has helped me to discard my victim mentality (my self-pity parties were based on me identifying myself as an orphan). A gratitude journal has been really easy to keep and I highly recommend it. At some stage of the day (usually in bed at night or first thing in the morning), I write down three things that I am grateful for. It does not need to be anything over the top, expensive or unique. I might simply be grateful for a beach walk or grateful to have enjoyed a nice coffee or meal.

If I am struggling to think of things to be grateful for, then it extends to simple luxuries such as a comfortable bed, access to running water, and so on. When you start doing this, your mindset changes and you start to feel grateful for so much more. As Voltaire says, *'Each player must accept the cards life deals him or her. But once they are in hand, he or she alone must decide how to play the cards in order to win the game.'*

SUMMARY

That brings us to the end of chapter six. In chapter seven, we delve into things that you can do to prioritise your mental health through your separation. But first, here's a summary of the key points discussed in chapter six:

> There are certain things that you can continue to be in control of. Identify and acknowledge these things and action them.

> If you feel like you need time out or extended periods of time to work through your separation, then take that time as best you can.

> Be organised – start keeping all of your documents and notes together, and also start a notebook detailing all relevant family law information.

> Arm yourself with knowledge in relation to both grief and loss, and also legal issues. Obtain legal advice (even if it's just free legal advice from your local legal aid office).

> It's business time! Put on your business hat and try to communicate with your ex-partner in a businesslike fashion.

> Try to avoid court if possible. Consider mediation and negotiation as alternatives.

- Recognise that some days will be more difficult than others. If you are having a 'good day', then use this time to be productive and attend to tasks that you have otherwise been putting off.

- If you need a lawyer, then consider engaging a fixed fee lawyer so that you stay more in control of your legal fees.

- Be grateful. Keeping a gratitude journal can help with this.

CHAPTER SEVEN

PRIORITISING YOUR MENTAL HEALTH

If you are reading this book, you are no doubt having a difficult time or have had a difficult time at some stage during your separation. I'm not pleased that you are struggling or have struggled in the past. But I am pleased that you are reading this book. It is important to acknowledge that the loss you have experienced is one of the most traumatic and painful things you will go through in your life. It's even harder if you're also dealing with the stress of protracted family law negotiations or litigation and the uncertainty of the family law system.

When you combine all of these factors, it can have a serious impact on your mental health. In fact, there is an increased risk of acute distress and depression following separation. Separation and divorce are commonly cited as a 'life event' that can trigger depression. Unfortunately, many people are ashamed to seek help or even acknowledge that they're struggling. But this can make it much, much worse. In the wake of a separation, it's critical that you prioritise your mental health. That's the focus of this chapter.

GETTING HELP COULD CHANGE YOUR LIFE

I did not know about the five stages of grief, as outlined in chapter three, until twelve months after my dad died. Given that my dad was a palliative care social worker, this seems ridiculous! I can honestly say that once I received some counselling and learned about the stages of grief, it completely changed my mindset. It helped me realise the *reason* I was feeling a certain way. It helped explain why I was behaving in certain ways at certain times. It helped me feel 'normal' and less alone with my feelings of loss.

Once I knew about the five stages of grief, I started searching for and purchasing many books on loss. This was the beginning of my research on Elisabeth Kübler-Ross's theory and, ultimately, the beginning of my journey in writing this book. (It was also ironic that when I began clearing out my dad's house and shed in order to sell his property, I started finding books on palliative care, loss and grief. Go figure!) But none of that would've happened if I hadn't received counselling to help me deal with the loss of my parents. Obtaining professional help was life-changing for me and it could be life-changing for you, too.

There are many counsellors and other mental health professionals who specialise in relationship breakdown counselling. There are also many generalist social workers and psychologists who will be able to assist you. I recommend many of my clients check in with their general practitioner to discuss their mental health and other effects that their loss may have had on their physical health.

Your general practitioner can write a mental health care plan for you, with a referral for a psychologist. The plan provides a number of free or subsidised sessions with that psychologist each year. A psychologist or counsellor can offer advice, guidance and coping mechanisms.

A number of the clients that I interviewed for this book sought assistance from psychologists and all described it as a positive experience. Similarly to myself, one client described it as life-changing. Another client, Dan, said that despite being a very resilient person, he felt as if his separation and family law experience were breaking him. He engaged in personal counselling to help him regain a sense of balance and 'reacquaint himself' with his resilience.

Sophie, who had been in a violent relationship, obtained a mental health care plan from her general practitioner and a referral to see a psychologist. Sophie completed sixteen sessions with the psychologist over a twelve-month period. His report confirmed that during the initial session, she was extremely anxious and depressed. However, at the time of writing his final report, he wrote, *'Her current presentation is that of a person who is now able to respond to life challenges and reflect on her mood and anxiety and make more appropriate and beneficial assessments of needed responses.'*

In addition to seeing a counsellor or psychologist, there may also be various support groups or specific counselling services that are relevant to you. Examples are domestic violence counselling or drug and alcohol counselling. If you are not already engaged with those types of counselling services, then your general practitioner and lawyer should be able to assist with a warm referral.

COURT CONSIDERATIONS

Seeking support for your mental health may also help you cope better if you have proceedings in court, particularly if they are protracted. I hope that you will be given additional tools from your mental health professional to deal with ongoing negotiations and/or litigation. They are the best person to discuss your particular concerns with, and can suggest different coping mechanisms to help you get through each stage of the proceedings.

Some clients have appointments booked with their mental health professional in the days leading up to a major event (such as a court hearing or meeting) and then also a pre-booked appointment the day after the event. Or you may receive tools from your mental health professional to help you deal with the loss you are experiencing, even if you were fortunate enough to have a relatively amicable breakup. These appointments and support may be more focused around grief and loss.

One thing to be mindful of when seeking professional mental health support is that, at some stage, if your matter does end up in the Family Law Courts, those medical records and notes may be subject to a subpoena. A subpoena is a document filed with the court, seeking information and records from somebody else (such as a medical professional). You should not worry about being criticised by the court for seeking assistance (in fact, often, the opposite is the case). However, the thought of your ex-partner having access to your personal counselling notes can be quite distressing for some clients.

KNOWING WHEN TO REACH OUT

At what stage should you reach out for support? Whenever you are ready or if you feel like things are starting to get on top of you. When speaking with child consultant and family dispute resolution practitioner Roxanne Nathan, she agreed that it is important not to let things fester. She gave this useful analogy:

> 'Separation is a spectrum; people do not realise they are unhappy and separate all on the same day. If you track separated relationships, you will often find a point where the first fracture happened. That fracture is often never fully repaired. I describe it as fracturing your leg and then you don't go to the doctor. You say, "It will be okay – I'll just walk with a limp for a while."

> 'Then time moves on and maybe your leg hurts a bit when it's cold, but you dismiss it and you say, "No, I won't got to the doctor – it will be okay." Then maybe you fracture it again and you still don't go and get support to really fix the fracture – you just keep struggling on. If the fracture is never repaired and more fractures happen, you just keep limping along until eventually your leg breaks and you can't walk anymore. That is then the point of separation. And that spectrum of time is different for each family.'

While this analogy highlights the importance of seeking support *before* you separate, it also applies to seeking support after a separation. If you ignore the pain or stress you're feeling, it'll only get worse.

My client Jillian consulted her general practitioner at a time when she felt incredibly stressed due to her separation and family law proceedings. She thought that she might have a problem with her heart, as she was having heart palpitations. Her doctor assured her there was nothing physically wrong with her heart. Rather, she was experiencing heart palpitations due to stress.

Poor mental health can lead to all sorts of mental and physical problems. Some people going through separation already have a mental illness, which adds further complications and difficulties to their personal situation. A mental illness is something that can be clinically diagnosed and includes things such as anxiety, depression, bipolar disorder and schizophrenia.

ANXIETY IN GRIEF

Feelings of anxiety during grief are normal. You may be experiencing anxiety even if you have never felt this type of emotion before. I personally experienced anxiety for the first time following the death of my parents. I'm an only child. At the time, I thought to myself, 'If both of my parents could die and I lose all of my family before I've even turned forty years old, then what else could happen?' I was scared!

There were days where I actually could not face leaving the house and there were other days where I needed to limit the amount of interaction I was having with other people. I still have the odd day now where I have an unexpected but very overwhelming sense of anxiety. Every now and then, I will be out in public and feel like I can't be there anymore. I have felt a sense of overwhelm and panic, have had difficulty breathing, and so on. Thankfully, this does not happen very often to me, but I had never experienced anything like this prior to my loss.

Some people are of the view that anxiety is the missing stage of grief. In fact, grief therapist Claire Bidwell Smith has written a book on that exact topic. It's titled *Anxiety: The Missing Stage of Grief*. In the book, Claire discusses her personal experience of grief after losing both of her parents before she turned twenty-five.

Afterwards, she became fearful of death, of flying and of all sorts of things that she had never previously feared. She describes anxiety as a way of protecting yourself: preparing for when the loss happens again. It is your mind trying to keep you safe. Anxiety can be exhausting and can also affect your sleep, which, in turn, can cause the anxiety to become worse. A mental health professional, such as a psychologist, can help you work through any anxiety you may be feeling.

DEALING WITH TRIGGERS

Have you noticed that seeing certain people, hearing certain music, smelling certain smells and going to certain places can sometimes trigger unpleasant feelings for you? Triggers are real and you need to be mindful of them.

The family home is often full of triggers. Family homes are not just real estate. They are often full of memories, both good and bad. There were likely wonderful times that you had with your ex-partner and perhaps your children there. In this way, the family home may be an emotional trigger. On the flip side, if there were traumatic events or negative experiences in that family home, this can also be triggering. If you're struggling to remain in the family home after your separation, then perhaps you should consider selling or renting out the property and living elsewhere.

My client Sophie took a while to be in a financial position to leave the family home. When she was finally able to, she said that it provided her with a sense of closure. Remaining in the home reminded her of the severe family violence that she was subjected to. Even the sound of stomping on the floorboards, or the sound that the front door made when closing, acted as a trigger. Sophie's ex-husband was also responsible for the death of her pet dog, who was buried in the front yard of the property. Sophie was relieved when she moved out of the family home, but it also caused a sense of sadness to leave behind her beloved dog.

Sophie also explained that when her ex-husband announced their marriage was over, one of the reasons he gave for leaving was along the lines of, 'I do not want to be stuck looking at you, next to me in the passenger seat of the car, for the rest of my life.' This caused Sophie considerable hurt and pain – to the extent that every time she got into the family car, it acted as a trigger, reminding her of those unkind words. Again, it took some time, but when Sophie was finally in a financial position to trade the car for a new one, it brought her happiness to no longer have that constant reminder.

Another client spoke about having to visit the local shopping centre for the first time post separation and feeling incredibly anxious about running into their ex-partner. My client Jillian said that she would avoid places she knew her ex-husband frequented. She also declined social invitations from mutual friends for the same reason. She was mindful of checking carparks for his car or scanning an area in case he might be there. She described feeling a *'pang of fear'* if she saw a car the same model or colour as his. Meanwhile, my client Dan said that whenever he drove past his old family home, it would remind him of the loss of the family unit and make him feel sad.

The family law process can also be triggering. Unfortunately for Sophie, when her matter ended up in court, the Family Law Court system required her to file affidavit material with incredible detail, including the history of family violence and her ongoing concerns to protect her children. Having to consult with me and to prepare her affidavits was quite traumatic for her. Likewise, reading what she perceived to be lies in her ex-partner's documents was also very upsetting for her.

Other triggers for Sophie included having to hand the children over at a supervised contact service, having to attend court hearings, and being in the same precinct as her ex-husband. Unfortunately, this was not negotiable and there was no option for her but to engage in the process.

This is not only concerning for victims of family violence. My view is that all parties having to attend court and be involved in the family law system are likely to be re-triggered in terms of their loss. For example, my client Jillian told me that she felt stressed throughout the entire process because she had to remember and write down all of the problems and trauma that she had experienced in the relationship.

I have assisted thousands of clients over the years. Most are usually displeased when receiving correspondence from another lawyer or reading affidavit material filed by their ex-partner. This can be re-traumatising or, at the very least, act as a trigger leading to other feelings of loss and grief. There is a lot to be said for avoiding litigation if at all possible. One method to help deal with this particular trigger was discussed in chapter six. That is, batching tasks. If at all possible, try to compartmentalise and batch tasks relating to your separation or family law matter. Remember my advice in relation to having a separate email address, so that you are not constantly triggered via your regular email address. Create yourself that space to avoid as many triggers as possible.

Often, the loss of a relationship can trigger feelings about losses from earlier in your life, particularly your childhood. According to Olivia Kay, the types of earlier losses that may be triggered include your own experience as a child of separated parents, or a previous relationship breakdown. Olivia says:

> *'Often, unresolved feelings relating to these prior losses will complicate an adult's response to their current situation, with emotional reactions to current difficulties reflecting these underlying feelings. For example, the breakdown of an adult relationship may bring to mind one partner's experience of emotional abandonment or disconnection from their parent during childhood, possibly prompting this adult to react in ways that are not congruent with the situation at hand, but rather reflect the emotional maelstrom underneath.'*

It is important to be mindful of these types of responses, which either yourself or your ex-partner may have, and recognise why they might be happening.

FRIENDS ARE NOT MENTAL HEALTH PROFESSIONALS

In her 1974 book, *Questions and Answers on Death and Dying*, Elisabeth Kübler-Ross discussed the principles of loss, which apply to those going through a separation. She stressed the importance of companionship. In particular, the importance of having someone sitting with you while you are going through those stages of loss and grief. This is very relevant to the loss that you may be experiencing.

Unfortunately, your friends and family may not know how to properly support you, or have the time to do it. Perhaps there was a period of 'busyness' after your separation, whereby your friends and family rallied around you, but now you feel forgotten. It doesn't mean that they don't care for you. However, they may not appreciate the ongoing pain of your loss or, even if they do, they may not know how they can help.

When experiencing grief from a death, the support often drops off once the funeral has passed. But the pain continues for those left grieving. The pain for you – as the months go on or as you continue through the family law system – will also continue, but the support will drop off. You may even find yourself sounding like a 'broken record' in relation to your separation, or that people get sick of hearing about it. In the meantime, this is fully consuming you.

The benefit of engaging a professional person is that they will sit and listen to you for as many months or years as needed. They are experienced and (hopefully) won't say the wrong things or simply try to 'fix' you (as we discussed in chapter four). They will not go away or lose concern. They will continue to provide you with support for as long as you want them to.

SEPARATION AND MEN'S MENTAL HEALTH

It would be remiss of me not to acknowledge the different ways that men and women cope upon their relationship breakdown. According to the World Health Organization, one person dies every forty seconds from suicide. What is the link between separation and suicide? Parents Beyond Breakup (PBB) works extensively with men who have separated from their partners. According to PBB, approximately ten to eleven men will suicide in Australia *each week* due to separation issues.

Children's custody issues specifically are said to account for approximately 100 male suicides each year. PBB is of the view that men in particular can become suicidal due to 'situational stress' arising from custody matters, the breakdown of a relationship and the loss of the family home.

According to Pete Nicholls, some of the most common feelings experienced by people who PBB assists are isolation and hopelessness, as many people feel there is no solution to what they are going through. (According to Pete, up to eighty-five per cent of the men who go to PBB for the first time have recently felt a sense of isolation – it is very common). Pete feels strongly that there is real value in people being able to tell *their story*. He says, *'Hearing another person's story is often the first time a person feels less isolated and alone. Sometimes, it allows them to realise that others are in a worse position.'*

PBB focuses on helping men cope with their situation by working to remove the feelings of hopelessness and isolation. The focus of the Dads in Distress branch of PBB is to allow men to get together as equals with their peers and to share their stories. Pete went on to tell me that, in his experience, men prefer to talk to others *'in the same boat'*, partly because it means they are on the same level; there is no feeling of hierarchy that men sometimes experience when speaking with an expert or professional. Here's a quote from one of the men who attends Dads in Distress (Pete described it as *'the best quote I've ever had from a dad'*):

> *'I have ugly emotional scars... I need to sit with and see other "ugly men", men damaged like me who've survived this, who can show me the way. I want someone that I know is not judging me, because I've lost trust in everything and everyone.'*

While Pete doesn't discount the value of speaking to a professional, he said that any help they can offer *'needs to work within and around [men] sitting with peers shoulder to shoulder'*. Pete says it's important to understand that men communicate differently. He recognises the importance of asking men the right questions, listening and sharing insight and wisdom, and *not* telling them what the answer is or what they *must* do.

If you are a female reading this book, then you may wonder how this section is relevant to you. If your ex-partner is male, then it may give you a better understanding of how you are both potentially dealing with your separation and loss. Having a better understanding of your ex-partner's journey will help you to better communicate and navigate your own journey.

SUMMARY

That brings us to the end of chapter seven. In chapter eight, I'll pinpoint specific ways to help you embrace the art of self-care – a key aspect of your separation journey. But first, here's a summary of the key points discussed in chapter seven:

> Do not be embarrassed to seek help – it could change your life. Please refer to the resource section at the back of this book if you would like or need some immediate assistance and support. I have included links to online mental health services and also telephone support.

> You may be experiencing anxiety for the first time in your life. Anxiety can be exhausting! It is not uncommon to be experiencing anxiety if you have suffered a loss.

> Recognise that there will likely be certain things that trigger you. How can you deal with these triggers? Are there places or people that you can avoid? If you have protracted legal negotiations or litigation, then you will have constant reminders of your loss.

> Your friends and family are likely well-meaning but they are not mental health professionals.

> Men and women will likely have different feelings around loss and grief. It is important to acknowledge the unique ways that men and women deal with separation.

CHAPTER EIGHT

EMBRACING THE ART OF SELF-CARE

You're probably wondering, 'What does a lawyer know about self-care?!' What I know is that I did not show myself much self-care during the really difficult periods of grieving the death of my parents.

In the deepest stage of loss and grief, particularly in the depression stage, you may not feel any sort of incentive for self-care. You may be having days where you do not want to get out of bed and you may feel as though you cannot achieve much for the day. Just getting through each day may feel absolutely draining. These flat days will likely reduce, but may come back from time to time.

You may have days or weeks where you are trying to juggle work, your separation and your children. On top of that, there may be the stress of the family law system. Have you been able to prioritise time for self-care during these difficult times? You may think it's not important in the grand scheme of things, or simply not possible. But I have seen first-hand the damage that clients can do to themselves, and their legal position, when they forget to look after themselves.

My client Dan felt that the separation from his partner, and not being able to see his son (as a result of false allegations against him), meant that there was never a day where he felt completely stress free. He said the anxiety he was experiencing on a daily basis resulted in him running at 'mid-strength' – although he was doing his best to mask this on a professional basis.

Ultimately, the consequence of Dan running at 'mid-strength' meant that he was not able to take on as much work and, indeed, his focus was not on growing his business. He said to me even recently that he really felt as though he could only fully and properly focus on one thing – either his business or his son. His son took priority and, as a result, his business and his bank account took a hit. It is only now, many months after final orders were made in court, that Dan feels as though he is able to put some energy back into his work.

If you don't look after yourself during this time, you too could find yourself running at mid-strength, which could have devastating consequences professionally as well as personally. As you know, I interviewed many clients and professionals in the process of writing this book. In this chapter, I'll share some of their key tips on self-care.

DIET AND EXERCISE

Without a doubt, if you can put aside time each day to exercise, then this is going to be of benefit to you. Your body is going through perhaps one of the most traumatic experiences ever. Exercise will reduce your body's stress hormones and, at the same time, will stimulate endorphins, which are 'feel-good' chemicals in the brain – a great stress-busting benefit! Study after study has highlighted the physical and mental benefits of exercise, including the direct link between exercise and stress relief.

My friend Rylie describes how he did not seek mental health support in relation to his separation, but did have a friend whom he spoke to regularly and who encouraged him to throw himself into his fitness. He says that starting to exercise has really motivated him and has helped him gain self-confidence. In fact, he will be running his first marathon this year! He now wakes at 5am instead of 7am to focus on his physical health.

My client Jane started walking regularly and spending time at the beach after her separation. She has also committed to weekly yoga, which she said is helping. Similarly, my client Sophie made a decision to walk as much as possible post separation. She said the combination of listening to music, getting outdoors and taking time out for herself on these walks was like therapy and became almost addictive. She also said, *'I remember the emotion I felt when I had to throw my sneakers away a few years later – they were a symbolic chapter of my life that was excruciating. I remember feeling gratitude for the mental and physical changes they had brought to me.'*

In addition to regular exercise, you also need to be mindful of what you eat. My client Jillian told me that she went on a chocolate and sugar 'bender' following her separation! She would also eat during the middle of the evening, which is something that she had not previously done. She found that she had put on a lot of weight throughout the process. She was also experiencing regular headaches and a stiff neck from stress, resulting in her relying on paracetamol on a regular basis. My client Dan also attributes eating more and poor eating habits to stress, which led to him going up a couple of pant sizes.

Similarly, I am the type of person who eats to excess when I am stressed or depressed. Needless to say, the kilos have piled on! I know, however, that many clients are the opposite in that they lose their appetite due to their grief and the stress that they are experiencing.

I recall an old client of mine who was in a terrible mental state during her court proceedings. It was not uncommon for her to shake from fear and anxiety while in court. There had been serious family violence during her relationship. She came back to our office around twelve to eighteen months after her matter had been finalised and we did not recognise her, as she looked just fabulous! She had lost weight thanks to healthier eating habits and regular exercise, and she was glowing as a result. She actually looked like a new person.

DRUGS AND ALCOHOL

Without a doubt, the biggest form of self-destruction for me has been my abuse of alcohol as I have worked through my losses. Regular consumption of wine became a daily habit for me for almost two years. I was using alcohol as a coping mechanism to mask the pain. My drinking did become a habit – I would get home after a day at hospital and immediately start drinking.

There came a point when I realised that stress was the trigger for my drinking; I distinctly remember walking out of one of the hospitals and, as soon as the doors opened, I was thinking of my next bottle of wine. If I was in the angry stage of grief, my drinking could be particularly damaging at times. I had been known to shoot off inappropriate or rude emails while drunk, or not have good judgement with personal social media updates. I was also diagnosed with alcoholic neuropathy, with some nerve damage. It seems drinking four-plus bottles of wine each week over a two-year period is *not* going to end well! I was masking my pain and my reality.

It was not easy, but I have since been able to change my relationship with alcohol and moderate my drinking. I decided that I did not want to drink to that extent, so I started reading books on addiction and alcohol reliance to help me better understand my triggers, and how alcohol was negatively affecting me. I was able to work through my alcohol reliance without the help of a professional or a drug and alcohol support service. However, if you feel that you would benefit from such support, your general practitioner will be able to assist you with a referral.

My client John disclosed that his alcohol habits became very bad to the point where he was using alcohol to try to calm himself. Upon reflection, he is now able to identify that it was actually making things worse for him. My client Dan also recalls suppressing stress with alcohol. It is certainly not uncommon.

I highly recommend using tools to help you redefine your relationship with alcohol (if you sense it's becoming a problem). There's an alcohol support app called Daybreak, created by Hello

Sunday Morning, which is a movement towards a better drinking culture. I recommend the app – which I myself have used – to help you better understand your drinking habits and/or reduce your alcohol consumption.

An interesting point to note is that even though you may be masking your pain through alcohol, or reaching out for help in a roundabout way via alcohol abuse, other people may justify your drinking. Your loved ones will likely recognise that you are going through a period of considerable stress and may use this as justification for your alcohol intake. While well-meaning, this is unlikely to be helpful for your physical or mental health. Again, if you feel as though you have become reliant on alcohol or are drinking more than you should, then I encourage you to seek support.

I also know a number of clients who use marijuana as a form of stress relief. In my experience, small amounts of marijuana use don't appear to have any real consequence in terms of parenting orders by the courts, as long as it is not in the presence of children.

However, I am saddened to say that in my close to twenty years of working as a family lawyer, I have seen an increase in the use of hard illicit drugs, such as ice and methamphetamine, which is incredibly sad to see. I have seen clients decline to the point that their addiction has resulted in their children being removed from them. I suspect, at times, their drug use was a way of coping by masking the feelings of loss. The consequences, however, will cause a much deeper level of loss and despair. Please seek immediate help from a professional if you have started using illicit drugs.

SLEEP AND STRESS

Have you had difficulty sleeping since your separation? Perhaps you are waking in the middle of the night and are unable to get back to sleep. You may be experiencing nightmares. You may be waking with anxiety. It cannot be emphasised enough how important it is for you to prioritise sleep. I am not recommending, nor am I qualified to recommend, sleeping tablets (that is something you may wish to discuss with your doctor). However, there are certain actions that you can take to try to give yourself the best opportunity to sleep – and sleep well.

I enjoy sleep meditation podcasts, which are available to download for free. You may want to play these in the background when you go to sleep. One app which I have found particularly helpful is called Calm, which includes evening mediations and bedtime stories for adults. Another tip is to remove your smartphone from beside your bed (or remove it from your bedroom altogether... I dare you!). You can also eliminate screen time for at least thirty minutes before going to bed, so as to ensure that your mind is not overly stimulated.

One of the other things I started doing when my mum was dying – and I was highly stressed – was using lavender oil. Lavender is known to have soothing and calming properties, and can apparently reduce stress. I now carry a small bottle of lavender oil in my handbag at all times. I highly recommend you try it, if you have not already, to help slow your thinking and to assist with your sleeping.

At times, when I felt incredibly stressed, I would rub it on my temples and also pop it on my pillow when trying to sleep. I was even splashing it about at the hospice when my mum only had days left to live. Understandably, I was not in the best mindset at that time, so I was trying anything at that point! But I really do believe that lavender has a calming effect. In fact, nowadays, the smell serves as a gentle reminder to be kind to myself. If I am feeling a little stressed, I pull it out of my handbag and take a few long breaths in through my nose. It is a very inexpensive method to help ease stress and potentially help you sleep.

If you are unable to improve your sleep, I suggest seeking some professional help from a sleep consultant.

MINDFULNESS AND MEDITATION

In the last few years, there seems to have been an increase in the number of businesses and service providers harping on about 'mindfulness'. Mindfulness has become such a buzzword! The truth is that there is actually a good reason for all the hype because mindfulness is so powerful. Mindfulness is particularly relevant if you are experiencing a loss, and also if you are feeling the stress of separation and/or the family law process.

The purpose of mindfulness is to bring your attention to whatever it is you are feeling. For example, you acknowledge and bring to the forefront of your mind the fact that you are feeling pain. It is about acknowledging the truth of the moment that you are in at the time – even when that moment hurts.

Today's society demands information and answers in a

'microwave minute'! Nobody seems to have the patience to wait for anything anymore; it certainly is the era of instant information and gratification. Practising mindfulness can help you shift this mindset. And one of the most popular ways to practise mindfulness is to meditate.

Meditation will help you to understand your thoughts at the time and to clear your mind. It can seem almost impossible to meditate when you are feeling immense stress. You may feel, at times, that you need to force yourself to meditate and you may need to persist with it. There are a number of apps that you can use to assist with mindfulness and beginner meditation. Calm, as mentioned earlier, is a really good starting point. If you search for 'meditation' on your podcast app, you'll see there are numerous others that you may find more appealing. Another wonderful resource is Doctor Elise Bialylew's Mindful in May website, which includes free guides, links to resources and also her book, *The Happiness Plan*, which I highly recommend.

Another tool that I strongly recommend is mindful breathing. This is a particularly good tool for those who are too impatient or resistant to trying meditation. Do not underestimate the power of taking five deep breaths in through your nose and out through your mouth. This mindful breathing technique can have an almost instant calming effect. I recommend trying it whenever you may be feeling some stress or anxiety. For example, prior to a telephone call with your ex-partner, prior to reading their emails, while reading correspondence from your lawyer or ex-partner, while at court, while attending a meeting in relation to your ex-partner, before you are due to see your ex-partner at a handover, or simply when you are feeling sad or anxious about your loss.

CRY, BABY

Crying is important. Many of the books and resources on loss and grief in the context of death refer to the importance of tears. They are natural and help to release the pain. Crying is an important part of the recovery process. It would not be uncommon for a memory, song or smell to make you cry and feel sadness about your loss. Personally, I will likely continue to feel sad at times and, often, it can be quite unpredictable.

While society wants to 'fix' your sense of loss and feelings of sadness, the grief that you are experiencing does not need to be fixed and there is no shame in crying. You should be able to sit with those tears and those feelings. You should be able to own those feelings. Allowing yourself to go through the pain does not mean that you wallow in self-pity or allow the pain to become your story. It is rather an acknowledgement of the way you are feeling at the time.

Megan Devine, in her book *(It's OK That You're Not OK)* and also via her website (Refuge in Grief), says that your pain needs space and room to unfold. I think this is why we seek out natural landscapes that are larger than us when we are feeling loss. She refers to the idea of 'limitless space' and the importance of entering these spaces away from other people. She refers to the trees not asking us questions about how we are feeling and the wind not caring if we cry.

For me personally, I find connection to the ocean and beach as a space where I can reflect and cry if need be without being judged. Often, the tears just come out while I am enjoying our beautiful natural environment. For you, it may be a nature walk or spending some time in your local park or botanic gardens. The benefits of time in nature, particularly without internet or devices, are quite remarkable.

SOCIAL MEDIA

There are both pros and cons of using social media when you have experienced a loss. One of the positives is that you are able to reach out to people in similar circles for support. For example, there are many social media groups focused on supporting separated families. There are groups aimed towards men and also women.

As a family lawyer, I have been a part of many of these groups, largely for observation to assist me in understanding the needs of my clients. One thing that is apparent is the sense of support and sense of community, in that people feel as though they have experienced similar types of loss.

If you feel as though you would benefit from a support group or engaging in these types of social media pages, then I would recommend setting up an anonymous account to do so. Section 121 of the *Family Law Act* (sorry to get technical!) precludes you from talking about any court matters. So if you are talking about your court matter, even in what seems to be a private group, you could be in trouble. Even if your matter is not in court, you never know who else is part of these online social groups. Someone may know your ex-partner or misinterpret contributions that you make to the group. Tread carefully.

I have already warned of the danger in using such support groups for legal advice. I can't stress enough the importance of using social media for support around issues of separation and loss rather than legal advice. I can tell you that some of the well-meaning legal 'advice' that I have seen in these forums and groups is absolutely wrong and/or damaging. I often cringe at the advice given.

For example, I often see plainly incorrect advice given in relation to parenting matters and what a realistic parenting agreement may look like. I also see 'advice' given around property settlements and the division of property, even though the people giving the advice have no idea of the facts of that particular relationship. Property settlements are very complex and there are so many factors that are unique to each particular matter. It is impossible to give blanket advice in a social media forum.

You can also use social media to express your feelings and emotions, and to reach out for support from your own network. As we experience a loss, it is not uncommon to reach out to people via social media for the ongoing expression and validation of our loss. It is easy for someone to send a quick DM, post an emoji sad face, or make a comment like 'Thinking of you' or 'Sorry to hear about that'. But as time goes by, the support you receive from your online 'friends' can also drop off. You can start feeling like a broken record when you post things about Father's Day, Mother's Day, birthdays and Christmas. It can be quite lonely when the 'likes' start to drop off and you are relying on the social media world for support.

Social media can also create a sense of jealousy. We all know the 'perfect family' on Instagram. These images can serve as constant reminders of the family unit you have lost. It can also be easy to compare yourself to others who have separated from their partners. How have they moved on so quickly? Why do they seem happy when you are in tears?

Ultimately, social media can be a great place for you to seek support and reach out for help, particularly if you are not comfortable asking for that help in 'real life'. But if social media is not serving you well, then you should take a break from it. Consider reducing your time on social media or having days where you are not checking the 'scroll hole' at all. I highly recommend it.

THE FAMILY HOME

The sense of loss around the family home is a loss that needs to be acknowledged. It may be that you have not been in a financial position to stay in the family home or that your ex-partner and the children have remained in the home so as to keep some consistency for the kids.

It can be emotionally overwhelming to say goodbye to a space. If the family home has to be sold, then this can cause further emotional difficulty and thoughts around who will be living in your space. Don't feel silly or embarrassed to grieve and feel a sense of loss around the family home. It is not uncommon, yet it is not something that is frequently acknowledged.

You are likely to go through some sort of decluttering process when moving homes or having your ex-partner leave the family home. This decluttering process can be excruciatingly difficult. Think carefully before your Marie Kondo-ing exercise (Marie Kondo is a professional organiser, known for her ruthless approach to eliminating clutter). Having cleared out my parents' house (by myself, no less), I know that it's a very painful experience. So many memories! Too much stuff to keep! There were things that I put in the skip that I regret and there were things that I sold that I wish I didn't. Once it is gone, it is gone.

If you are not ready or not in the right mindset, then leave it until later if you can. Unfortunately, this process is often driven by a timeline, such as leaving or selling a house, so your hand may be forced to do this sooner rather than later.

Lawyers are often quick to put a value on household contents for the purpose of negotiating a property settlement, but the reality is that many household contents will hold special memories for you. My client John was able to remain in the family home post separation and he retained most of the household contents. He told me that he had not disposed of anything because it meant there would always be positive memories of his relationship.

However, I have read that a good cull or cleanout can help you to let go of resentment and pain, which you are likely feeling post separation. It can also help to remove bad memories and savour the special memories. If you have children, then avoid being too ruthless as they may appreciate some of the things you are considering throwing out when they become older. You may even want to create a time capsule full of meaningful items for the children, as a way of cherishing special memories of the home. My view is that it is easiest to do the Marie Kondo cull while in the acceptance stage of your loss and grief.

OTHER SUGGESTIONS

In this chapter, we've spoken at length about the importance of forming healthy habits. Each habit – whether it's exercising, meditating or simply being in nature – should be a positive habit that you commit to daily, knowing that you will feel better afterwards. But as part of your self-care, you should also think about planning things to look forward to, such as a holiday or a special dinner. Forward planning and creating small goals can help to give your mind focus and direction. It also ensures that you have things to look forward to and that you are setting the time aside to really look after yourself.

This is particularly important on days that you might find more difficult than others. For me, Father's Day and Mother's Day can be tough. For you, it might be Christmas Day and Valentine's Day, as these are days you used to enjoy with your partner. Having a plan in place will really help you get through those days. It could be as simple as planning a special lunch, going to the movies, spending time with your loved ones, doing something extravagant or doing absolutely nothing at all. It really depends on you and *your* needs.

Also, as a way of marking the end of the relationship, you may like to host some sort of gathering or even a divorce party. To some, this will sound tacky. Others will really appreciate the process of remembering the relationship and the family unit. You may like to create a box of memorabilia to remember the good parts of the relationship. You may want to bury things that you love (or hate!). You may want to plant a tree in memory. You may want to burn a pile of belongings! There are all sorts of things that you can do, but really it comes down to what feels right for you as you grieve your loss.

My client Sophie experienced a further sense of loss when she discovered that the frozen embryos she and her ex-husband had created together through an extensive IVF process had to be thawed due to unpaid storage fees. She purchased a tree and buried the embryos under that tree. This is a really special and memorable thing to do. You can apply this idea to anything that held meaning for you in the relationship.

SUMMARY

That brings us to the end of chapter eight – and almost the end of the book. Before I share my final thoughts with you, here's a summary of the key points discussed in chapter eight:

> Embracing the art of self-care involves acknowledging your loss and taking care of yourself – physically, mentally and emotionally – as best you can.

> There are numerous ways that you can practise self-care during these difficult times, including being mindful of your diet and exercise, limiting your consumption of alcohol, practising methods for a peaceful sleep to enable you to

recharge your body, and allowing yourself to cry. You may also wish to try meditation and the practice of mindfulness, if you have not previously.

> Use social media wisely – there are some great support groups but beware of any legal advice given by anyone who is not a lawyer. Also, if you sense social media is doing more harm than good, consider reducing or eliminating the time you spend on it.

> Acknowledge the sense of loss you may feel in relation to the family home, and try to avoid decluttering or clearing it out until you're in the acceptance stage of loss and grief.

CONCLUSION

AN OPPORTUNITY TO GROW

'Muddy water, let stand, becomes clear.'
– Lao Tzu

Hopefully, by now, you have a better understanding around the loss that you have endured as a result of your separation. I hope that you have a better understanding of *why* you feel certain emotions or have acted in certain ways.

Are you able to take a step back and reflect on your behaviour and how you have conducted yourself? I am talking about how you have conducted yourself in terms of your dealings with your ex-partner and others, such as your friends, family members, service providers or any random member of the public. Are you pleased with the way that you have conducted yourself or does your reflection cause you embarrassment in some cases?

My client Sophie told me that when she consulted with a psychologist, she was asked to come up with two words to uphold throughout the separation process. The words that she chose were dignity and grace. I think those words chosen by Sophie, and the decision she made to conduct herself that way, are to be commended.

But that doesn't mean it's easy. Far from it!

SOME DAYS ARE JUST SHIT

Let's get real here. No matter what supports you have in place and no matter how much self-care you have invested in yourself, some days are just… *shit!* After your separation, you may have days where you are able to engage with others, be productive and even laugh (a 'good day'). However, you might wake up the following morning and know immediately that it won't be a good day. Some days, you may simply need to sit with your feelings of deep sadness rather than trying to push them aside.

Please remember that loss and grief are not something that you need to 'get through'. You do not need to rush through the way that you are feeling and you certainly do not need to rush through each stage of grief. Indeed, you may not even experience *any* of the stages of grief – and that's okay. Your loss is unique.

At this point, I would like you to consider which stages (if any) you think you may have experienced, or whether any of them resonate with you at the moment. I also recommend re-reading this book in, say, three to six months, as your situation and mindset will likely be different to how you are feeing today. In his book *The Subtle Art of Not Giving a F*ck*, Mark Manson talks about radical change and how our perspective differs following our worst moments. It is true that no matter what stage you are at while reading this book, your perspective is likely different to how it was immediately following the separation, and it will likely be different again in six or twelve months' time.

YOU GET TO CHOOSE HOW YOU NAVIGATE YOUR LOSS

> *'With everything that has happened to you, you can either feel sorry for yourself or treat what has happened as a gift. Everything is either an opportunity to grow or an obstacle to keep you from growing. You get to choose.'*
> – Doctor Wayne Dyer

The key points that I hope you'll remember from this book are:

- Each loss is different and unique.

- Even amicable separations are difficult – and it is okay to feel a sense of loss.

- Your loss may not be easier just because you initiated the separation.

- Time itself does not heal. Rather, it is what you do in that time that will make the difference.

- The cliché of 'keeping busy' and putting your emotions to the side is flawed. You should be able to feel whatever emotion you are feeling without the need to 'get over' those thoughts. You should be able to sit with your feelings.

Family consultant Artemicia Nisyrios shared these words with me when I asked for any tips for you, the reader, to help effectively manage your emotions:

> 'Acknowledge that separation and family law is one of the most difficult things anyone can ever face and that it is "normal" to be feeling grief and loss.'

It is ultimately in your hands to acknowledge that you have experienced a loss. Once you do, the concepts of loss and grief, and the emotions attached to them, will make much more sense to you. It's not so much about trying to *recover* from the loss but rather having and using tools to *navigate* your loss.

Remember, your loss and grief are not something to be 'managed'. While this book has explored some theory and concepts around grief, I am in no way suggesting that your experience is black and white or that there's a set of rules you must follow. There is no 'getting over' your pain. You need to feel it to heal it. There is no timeline and there is no right way. You need to grieve and feel your loss your way.

My client Jillian told me that when she was at her worst, she would remind herself of the Persian adage: *'This too shall pass.'* The loss and grief you're feeling are not likely to pass entirely, but will evolve and hopefully become easier to bear.

I wish you all the best on your journey.

HELPFUL RESOURCES

LIFELINE

lifeline.org.au | 13 11 14
24-hour crisis support and suicide prevention services

ANGLICARE AUSTRALIA

Anglicare offers parenting courses such as 'Kids Are First' and 'Mums and Dads Forever Program'. Each state offers different courses and support, so search for Anglicare in your particular state.

BEYOND BLUE

beyondblue.org.au | 1300 22 4636
Mental wellbeing assistance, including 24/7 telephone support and online support.

CIRCLE OF SECURITY INTERNATIONAL

circleofsecurityinternational.com
Resources for parents, including Circle of Security Parenting program.

FAIR WORK OMBUDSMAN

The Fair Work Ombudsman provides information on family and domestic violence leave: **https://www.fairwork.gov.au/leave/family-and-domestic-violence-leave**

FAMILY RELATIONSHIP CENTRES

familyrelationships.gov.au
Post separation support and family dispute resolution (mediation) services.

HEADSPACE

headspace.com
Mindfulness for everyday life, including a mediation app.

HELLO SUNDAY MORNING

hellosundaymorning.org
Hello Sunday Morning has a mission to change the world's relationship with alcohol. One of its offerings is Daybreak – a free app and anonymous online community, designed to help people change their drinking habits.

MENSLINE AUSTRALIA

mensline.org.au | 1300 78 99 78
MensLine is a free telephone and online counselling service for men, including relationship breakdown and parenting support.

MINDFUL IN MAY

mindfulinmay.org
Meditation and mindfulness resources.

MINDSIGHT

mindsight.net.au
Mindsight, led by Artemicia Nisyrios, provides family counselling and psychological services. Artemicia also writes family reports for the Family Law Courts. (Thank you to Artemicia, who was interviewed for *Separate Ways*. Her commentary has been referred to throughout the book.)

NATIONAL LEGAL AID

nationallegalaid.org
Each state administers legal aid to assist clients who cannot afford legal representation. You can search the National Legal Aid website to find the legal aid commission in your state.

PARENTS BEYOND BREAKUP & DADS IN DISTRESS

parentsbeyondbreakup.com | 1300 853 437

Parents Beyond Breakup is a specialised suicide prevention charity, with the tagline 'Keeping parents alive, and in their kids' lives'. Services include online support and face-to-face support groups around Australia. (Special thanks to CEO Peter Nicholls, who was interviewed for *Separate Ways*. His commentary has been referred to throughout the book.)

RELATIONSHIPS AUSTRALIA

relationships.org.au

Relationships Australia offers support for families, including relationship advice, family dispute resolution (mediation) and parenting/education programs.

RENEWAL COUNSELLING

renewalcounselling.com.au

Renewal Counselling is led by Paul Ellis, who offers a variety of counselling services, including relationship counselling, and support for those dealing with grief and loss. (Thank you to Paul, who was interviewed for *Separate Ways*, and provided some valuable ideas and input.)

THE ADELAIDE RESOLUTION CENTRE

theadelaideresolutionscentre.com.au

The Adelaide Resolution Centre assists families who have separated. It provides family assessments, therapy and also dispute resolution services. (Thank you to Olivia Kay, who was interviewed for *Separate Ways*, and provided some invaluable tips and commentary.)

ACKNOWLEDGEMENTS

THE CONCEPT FOR THIS BOOK HAS BEEN IN MY MIND FOR THE PAST two years. I am chuffed to have now finally reached the point of publication, and I'm very pleased to be sharing my ideas around grief in the context of family law and separation. Writing Separate Ways has been a very emotional and, at times, difficult journey due to my own sense of loss and grief.

A special thanks to Tom Donaghy of Tom Donaghy Partners who was the first person to teach me about the five stages of grief after my dad died and while my mum was dying. Tom transformed my mindset and my life. Learning about the stages of grief opened my eyes and my heart, and I no longer felt like I was going crazy. Tom's coaching has left a lasting impact on me, to making me re-think the way I work with clients, and really listen to their stories of loss and grief in the context of separation. I cannot thank you enough, Tom.

Thank you to those who have contributed to this book, including those experts who work with separated families. I have included references to these interviews throughout the book and have also noted your contact details in the reference section. Your experience and input have been invaluable.

I particularly want to thank my current and past clients who were brave enough to share their stories in such a raw and honest way. Your stories and your words of wisdom will no doubt assist the reader during their own personal journey.

Thank you to Elham Rabbah and my team at The Family Law Project. I often come up with crazy ideas, such as writing a book, and you sometimes allow me to pursue these crazy ideas!

Thank you to my husband, Shane, for your support throughout the book-writing process and your support through my journey of grief and loss. It has been very difficult at times but you have always stuck by me.

Finally, it would be remiss of me not to thank my dad and my mum. I miss you both so much and I know that you would be proud of me for having written this book.

About the Author

Shaya Lewis-Dermody is a specialist family lawyer with almost twenty years of experience. She has worked with thousands of family law clients across Australia and also New Zealand. She is also regularly appointed by the court to act as an Independent Children's Lawyer in complex custody disputes.

In 2019, Shaya was a finalist in the national Women in Law Awards, in the category of Thought Leader of the Year. She has also been voted by her peers as a Doyle's Guide leading lawyer.

Shaya is the owner and principal solicitor of The Family Law Project, which is a socially responsible and progressive family law firm, with a focus on access to justice. Shaya started the law firm following her frustration over the lack of quality and accessible family law services. There was also a gap in the market in terms of fixed fee lawyers.

Shaya is regularly featured as a thought leader in her field, having conducted media interviews with ABC Radio, The Saturday Paper, Domain and many more.

To find out more about THE FAMILY LAW PROJECT, visit:
www.familylawproject.com.au
You can also find The Family Law Project on Facebook (www.facebook.com/familylawproject).

CPSIA information can be obtained
at www.ICGtesting.com
Printed in the USA
BVHW061003090920
588371BV00002B/104